One Fantastic Ride

One Fantastic Ride

The Inside Story of Carolina Basketball's

2009 Championship Season

Adam Lucas, Steve Kirschner, and Matt Bowers

WITH A FOREWORD BY ROY WILLIAMS

Jeffrey A. Camarati, Photo Editor

THE UNIVERSITY OF NORTH CAROLINA PRESS   CHAPEL HILL

Designed and set by Kimberly Bryant in The Serif,
Gotham, and Champion types
Manufactured in the United States of America

*The paper in this book meets the guidelines for
permanence and durability of the Committee on
Production Guidelines for Book Longevity of the
Council on Library Resources.*

*The University of North Carolina Press has been a
member of the Green Press Initiative since 2003.*

Danny Green photo (right) by Jeffrey A. Camarati;
Ty Lawson photo (p. vi) by Peyton Williams.

Library of Congress Cataloging-in-Publication Data
Lucas, Adam, 1977–
One fantastic ride : the inside story of Carolina
basketball's 2009 championship season / Adam
Lucas, Steve Kirschner, and Matt Bowers.
    p. cm.
Includes bibliographical references.
ISBN 978-0-8078-3385-8 (cloth : alk. paper)
1. University of North Carolina at Chapel
Hill—Basketball. 2. North Carolina Tar Heels
(Basketball team) 3. NCAA Basketball Tournament.
I. Kirschner, Steve (Steven A.) II. Bowers, Matt.
III. Title.
GV885.43.U54L85 2009
796.323'6309756565—dc22   2009027707

cloth   13 12 11 10 09   5 4 3

My hat's off to the guys in our locker room,

because they took me on one fantastic ride,

and it's something I'll never forget.

—ROY WILLIAMS, April 7, 2009

Contents

Foreword

I often tell my players to enjoy the journey—meaning that I don't want them to just look at the results at the end of the year. A basketball season, like life, has its ups and downs, its challenges and rewards. Too often, society judges only the outcome and not the series of steps that make up the journey.

This championship season was the toughest in which I have ever coached. Of course, the pressure that comes with lofty expectations was placed on our team before practice even began. But we always have pressure at Carolina, and this year our players managed it amazingly well. In fact, they thrived on it.

So it was not the pressure that made the season so tough, but rather the injuries to key personnel. There were too many days when I wondered whether I should cut a drill short or risk further injury to Tyler Hansbrough's shin, or Marcus Ginyard's foot, or Ty Lawson's toe. There were days when we had more guys riding exercise bikes than running sprints.

But we made it through those tough times, and through hard work and unselfish play, we became the team I hoped we would be. I was so proud to see our players make individual sacrifices to help this team reach its goals. They matured and improved, and along the way, many of them shed the labels people had given them.

The so-called experts said Ty Lawson was soft, but he developed a toughness and a will to win that became an unstoppable force as he emerged as the best point guard in the country.

They said Wayne Ellington was just a jump shooter, but he became an outstanding all-around player and the Final Four MVP.

They said Bobby Frasor was done after two injury-shortened seasons, but he became our best defensive player.

They said Danny Green danced too much, but he saved his best basketball for last and made sure he will be remembered for his game and not just his enthusiasm.

And they said Tyler Hansbrough was overrated. The big fella laughed when he heard that, but we knew deep down it fueled his passion to excel. His number 50 jersey was already going to be retired, and he could have shot 25 times a game to stay in the National Player of the Year race. Instead, he chose to

continue to play in an unselfish, team-first way. He understood that Lawson, Ellington, Green, Deon Thompson, Ed Davis, and others could help him get what he wanted most: a national championship banner in the Smith Center. By doing so, Tyler will be remembered as one of the best to ever play our game.

For many of the players, the championship was the culmination of three or four years of hard work together. What began with a preseason trip to the Bahamas over Labor Day weekend in 2005 ended with cutting down the nets four years later in Detroit. In between were many great victories, a few agonizing defeats, hundreds of practices, and so many moments I will cherish forever.

To watch these young men accomplish what they worked so hard for was an absolute joy and a coach's dream. It was, in the truest sense, One Fantastic Ride.

Roy Williams

Prologue June

North Carolina's 2009 national championship season unofficially began on April 24, 2008. That was the day that Roy Williams could not persuade Tyler Hansbrough to leave the Smith Center weight room long enough to craft a statement announcing Hansbrough's intention to turn down millions of NBA dollars and return for his senior season at Carolina.

This would be the third time at Carolina that Hansbrough had decided against turning professional and the third time he had declined to create any kind of fanfare around his decision. As a freshman and a sophomore, he had announced his intention to return within ten days of the end of the Tar Heels' season. The first time, he did it with a simple press release. The second time, he made his announcement at the postseason team-awards ceremony.

His third decision took a little longer and was slightly more difficult. He was the consensus National Player of the Year. He was only the third unanimous Atlantic Coast Conference Player of the Year in league history. He was only the fifth Tar Heel to twice win consensus All-American recognition.

The awards and the stats suggested it was time for Hansbrough to leave. Mock drafts had slotted him somewhere between the 16th and 20th picks of the NBA Draft's first round; those draft positions guaranteed that he would earn between $6.4 million and $5.3 million over the next four years.

There were two problems, however. First, Hansbrough loved college. The day after telling Williams about his decision, he would join fellow rising seniors Bobby Frasor and Marcus Ginyard (whose participation somehow remained clandestine despite a flurry of national attention) in leaping from the balcony of the Sigma Alpha Epsilon fraternity house into a swimming pool. The jump made ESPN's *SportsCenter* and filled local talk radio airwaves. It was called irresponsible and dangerous by some.

Hansbrough called it fun. What he realized, and what everyone else seemed to miss, was that the actual jump was no big deal; people were in a frenzy simply because there were *photos* of the jump. Without the photos, there was

no story—there was just a typically crazy end-of-semester college party, and Hansbrough was a college kid who liked to have fun.

What he liked even more, though, was winning—the second reason that made leaving college early so difficult. He was forced to acknowledge that if he left now, his final memory of his Tar Heel career would be walking off the Alamodome court after an 84–66 waxing by Kansas in the Final Four. It was just the 18th defeat of his class's college career, but it was the worst. Thirteen minutes into the game, the Jayhawks had led 40–12.

"The Kansas game was such a factor in my coming back," Hansbrough said. "It's one of those feelings where you get so close to something that you dream about when you're a kid, and then it just all ends. It wasn't a close game at all. We pretty much got blown away, and to go out like that and get manhandled in front of everybody on a big stage, that was a motivating factor."

It motivated him so much, in fact, that his head coach couldn't even get him to stop lifting weights to discuss the matter.

"You're sure?" Williams asked the reigning National Player of the Year. "And you've talked about it with your parents?"

"I'm sure," said Hansbrough, who was working out with Tar Heel strength-and-conditioning coach Jonas Sahratian.

"We need a statement," Williams said. "You need to say something."

Hansbrough paused just long enough to look irritated.

"Just say something you think I would say," he said, and he went back to his workout.

FOR THREE OTHER TAR HEELS, the decision would not be so simple. On the same day the news broke that Hansbrough would return for his senior season, Ty Lawson and Wayne Ellington announced they would enter the NBA Draft without hiring an agent, which made them eligible to return to school if they withdrew their names before June 16. One day later, Danny Green also submitted his name for draft consideration.

For the next two months, Williams had no idea what the composition of his 2008–09 team might be. If everyone returned, his Tar Heels would be loaded and the consensus preseason national title favorite. If all three players bolted, his team would not even be the preseason conference favorite. Approximately four weeks later, he signed Durham product Justin Watts to a letter of intent as perimeter depth insurance in case of a mass departure.

Meanwhile, he was dealing with his other returning players, who would certainly form a very good team, although he had no idea if they still had the potential to be a great team.

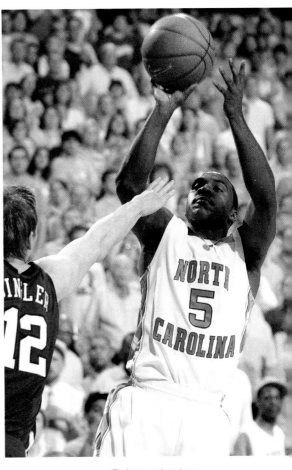

Ty Lawson's return helped make UNC the preseason favorite. (Photo by Jeffrey A. Camarati)

"I don't know if they're going to be with us," Williams told Ginyard, Frasor, and the others. "It's a process, and we've got to let them go through it."

The returning players were aware that the team's fortunes hinged on the NBA decisions. "There was some concern from their teammates, and we talked about it openly," Williams said.

By Memorial Day, the trio's futures were still unclear. Williams stayed in close contact with NBA general managers and coaches, gauging the likelihood that any of his three players would move into the magical lottery part of the first round. Lawson was the most sought after of the three players, with all Williams's contacts assuring him that Lawson would be a first-round pick and possibly a lottery selection.

"But will you pick him if he's available?" Williams asked several teams.

Summertime Battles

It was March 2009, just days before Carolina's opening-round NCAA Tournament game against Radford, and sounds of a heated dispute filled the Tar Heels' locker room in the basement of the Smith Center.

"We're the better team, definitely more talented," junior Deon Thompson said.

"No way, look at it player by player and it's obvious," countered 2005 graduate and NCAA champion Melvin Scott. "Plus, until y'all win that ring, you can't say anything."

Thompson protested, but he knew Scott was right. It was an argument that dated to pickup games the previous summer.

When Wayne Ellington, Danny Green, and Ty Lawson withdrew from the NBA Draft, the 2008–09 Tar Heels were immediately hailed as potentially one of the best teams in college basketball history. But in pickup games against former Tar Heel players like Scott, Jawad Williams, Sean May, and Marvin Williams, the current team couldn't argue much with the '05 bunch, which proudly pointed to its banner in the Smith Center rafters.

"There's no question that during the summer, whether it was the camp-counselor game or seeing the guys' faces after they were done with that game playing the old guys, there was a focus and a single vision for this team," said director of basketball operations Jerod Haase.

The quest to quiet the players from Roy Williams's first national title team began as soon as Carolina lost to Kansas in the 2008 Final Four, and it hit full stride in workouts with Jonas Sahratian, the team's strength-and-conditioning coordinator, during summer school.

"After the KU game, it left a bitter taste in everybody's mouth, but it set the tempo for what we needed to work on for the off-season with everybody," Sahratian said. "For all the players, it was their first taste of the Final Four, so they were eager to get back there and try to win the whole thing. There was a lot of motivation to hit the ground running and have a really productive off-season."

Sahratian has developed a reputation as one of the best in his field by putting his charges through a sometimes brutal routine that includes Olympic weight lifting, squatting, running hills, pushing oversized truck tires, and more. Another of his favorites is Danneyball, a version of volleyball played with a 10-pound medicine ball that improves conditioning and lateral change of direction.

The Kansas loss hit Tyler Hansbrough so hard that he was back the next day working with Sahratian, preparing for his last run at an NCAA championship. He added the habit of making 250 to 300 jump shots a day to his normal regimen in the weight room.

"I think the loss was a motivating factor . . . pretty much throughout the preseason, working out in the weight room with Jonas," Hansbrough said. "That was a big factor for everybody."

"I think if you look at every year I have been here, each year we have gotten better," said junior Deon Thompson. He agreed that losing to Kansas, as well as to Georgetown in the 2007 Elite Eight, inspired the players to work even harder. "The way we lost on the biggest stage in college basketball really fueled us all summer."

Deon Thompson in summer workouts. (Photo by Jeffrey A. Camarati)

A few weeks after the Kansas loss, the returning Tar Heels hit the ground running. The upperclassmen did not want to waste the rare opportunity to pursue a championship with such a talented and experienced team.

"I think the driving factor throughout the year was that not many times does a team get to have juniors and seniors who come back for three [or] four years to win a national championship," senior Bobby Frasor said. "I definitely could say that we were more experienced, more focused—any adjective you want to use to describe it—from day one in the off-season."

Ellington, Green, and Lawson weren't in town for the early summer sessions as they traveled to workouts around the country before pulling out of the NBA Draft. Once they returned to Chapel Hill, the hard work for 2009 began.

"Those guys that weren't there might've been doing basketball workouts, but they weren't doing the strength training, the flexibility work, the speed development, all of those things," Sahratian said. "They were a little bit behind. When they came back, it was, 'Hey, we've got to make up for lost time.' When they finally did get back, everything was fine."

Marcus Ginyard's summer preparations were derailed by foot injuries that lingered through the season. (Photo by Jeffrey A. Camarati)

To team members who hadn't toyed with NBA possibilities, the transition was smooth.

"The day that Danny and Wayne came back, we had a pickup game in the Smith Center, and I didn't feel like anything had changed," said senior Patrick Moody.

With the NBA flirtations behind them, all the Tar Heels were united again from the off-season until the night of April 6 in Detroit's Ford Field.

"When it's all said and done, there was one goal in mind," Haase said. "As great as the ACC championship is, as great as Maui is, as great as the Final Four was the previous year, there was a single purpose, and that was winning the national championship. Everybody was completely together with that. There were no other ulterior motives. Everybody understood that the better the team did, the better they would do individually."

And, as the players realized, the better the team did, the quicker the 2009 Tar Heels could end the taunting of their counterparts from 2005.

"All of that hard work we put in paid off, and we won the championship," Lawson said. "The 2005 guys can't say anything else to us because they always used to point at the banner . . . when we would beat them in pickup games. They can't do that anymore."

Roy Williams at the 2008 College World Series. (Photo by Minorwhite Studios)

None of the general managers would guarantee the pick. Further complicating matters for the not-quite-21-year-old Lawson was a traffic stop made by the police as he was driving home one night in early June. He was stopped for playing his music too loud, then cited for driving after drinking while being under age. National headlines, seen by every NBA team, implied that he was driving while impaired, although in reality he registered nowhere near the limit on the blood-alcohol test. But the incident added to the stress of making a career decision with a deadline fast approaching. (In August, Lawson was ordered to perform 26 hours of community service for the misdemeanor.)

Uncertainty about their pro futures eventually led Lawson, Ellington, and Green to decide to return to school. Williams received the news just before departing on a flight to Omaha to watch the Carolina baseball team in the College World Series. Upon returning to Chapel Hill, he met with each of the three players. He had two goals: he wanted to make sure that they were coming back for the right reasons and that, if they did come back, they understood his expectations.

"From the first day, I told them, 'It's not going to be about you getting 30 shots,'" Williams said. "'It's not going to be about focusing on you and doing what some NBA scout thought you needed to do. It's going to be about our team.'"

He got exactly the reaction he was hoping for.

"The kids looked at me, like, 'Coach, I'm surprised you even said that.'"

At that moment, Williams ceased being their adviser and returned to being their head coach. He had spent two months preparing them for a possible professional future. Now it was his job to reacquaint them with the idea that they were once again Tar Heels, with all the expectations that came with that title.

"You're eight weeks behind everybody," he told Green, Lawson, and Ellington. "You're going to have to bust your tails to catch up. And you've got to get involved with your teammates. . . . You've got to really work."

While the draft testers had been crisscrossing the country, going to job interviews and draft camps, their teammates had continued the regular Carolina summer routine: an early-afternoon workout with Sahratian followed by late-afternoon pickup games. Those games often included former Tar Heels now in the NBA who were visiting Chapel Hill—players like Marvin Williams, Shammond Williams, Sean May, and Raymond Felton.

Once the news became official, Ellington, Lawson, and Green immediately rejoined those games. Before they could be reintegrated into the team, however, some frank discussions needed to take place.

"We were extremely direct with each other," Ginyard said. "We had to be very direct with each other to be assured that everybody had the same goal

in mind and understood we have the potential to reach that goal if we were all focused and on the same page. We couldn't take that first step until we all knew everybody was in it together to make a championship run."

"Tyler, Marcus, and I were worried about whether they would have Carolina as their first interest," Frasor said. "Credit to Coach Williams, because from day one, that was never an issue. Throughout the whole year, I don't think anyone questioned that they were playing for . . . the name on the front on the jersey, not the back."

"I understood where everyone was coming from," Ellington said. "We'd been gone so long while we were trying to make our decisions. If one of my teammates did that, I'd wonder whether he wanted to be here playing with us or not."

On the night of June 16, Ellington, Green, and Lawson walked back into the Smith Center. A pickup game was in progress, so they would have to wait to get back on the court. The first teammate to spot them was Ginyard.

He greeted them with a wide smile and a mock inquisition.

"Hey guys," he said. "And where have you been all summer?"

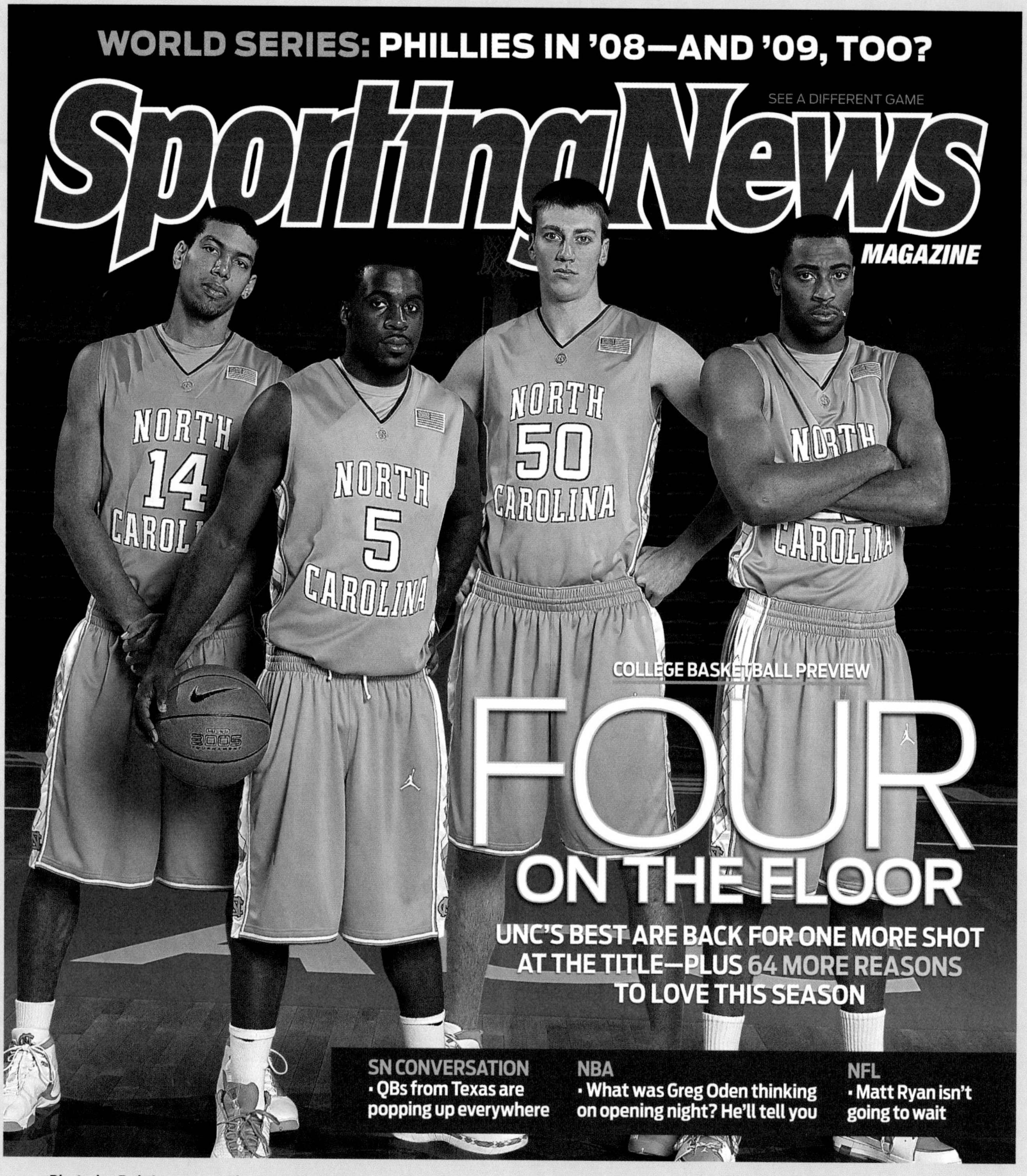

WORLD SERIES: PHILLIES IN '08—AND '09, TOO?
SEE A DIFFERENT GAME
SportingNews
MAGAZINE
NORTH 14 CAROLI
NORTH 5 CAROLINA
NORTH 50 CAROLINA
NORTH CAROLINA
COLLEGE BASKETBALL PREVIEW
FOUR
ON THE FLOOR
UNC'S BEST ARE BACK FOR ONE MORE SHOT AT THE TITLE—PLUS 64 MORE REASONS TO LOVE THIS SEASON
SN CONVERSATION
• QBs from Texas are popping up everywhere
NBA
• What was Greg Oden thinking on opening night? He'll tell you
NFL
• Matt Ryan isn't going to wait

Photo by Bob Leverone, *The Sporting News*

Opening Day

The prevailing assumption was simple: the 2008–09 Tar Heels would just pick up where last year's edition left off, pulverize opponents, and cruise to the national championship.

Players and coaches—all players and coaches, anywhere in the world of basketball—knew better. Every team is different. Every team is an independent organism, one that begins its life on the first day of practice and develops over the course of the season. Many of the 2009 faces would be the same, but beloved senior Quentin Thomas had graduated and freshmen Ed Davis, Larry Drew II, Tyler Zeller, and Justin Watts had been added. Will Graves was a sophomore expected to have a significantly expanded role.

It was still a very good team. But it was a different team.

"This team had to reinvent itself," director of basketball operations Jerod Haase said. "You look at it quickly and you assume it's pretty much the same team as last year. Just go from one season to the next and add four great freshmen. But it was a situation where we were really in flux for a while. From the end of the season, the loss to Kansas, until the start of the next season, a lot of things changed. It really was reinventing the team from the start rather than just assuming everything would pick up like last year."

The coaching staff expected the reinvented Tar Heels to have one major asset: depth. The top six scorers returned from the 2008 squad, and Davis, Drew II, and Zeller were very highly recruited. Add Graves and the rotation looked ten deep.

Then the injuries began. Marcus Ginyard had suffered an ankle injury in midsummer that forced him to hobble on crutches for four weeks. When he finally ditched the crutches, he noticed something that concerned him: the foot injury he'd played through as a junior still hurt.

"I had been off of it for almost a month and a half," Ginyard said. "When it was still hurting, that made me think something wasn't right. I got it checked out, went through a series of different tests, and realized I had a stress frac-

ture. And at the end of August, we had to make a decision about what we were going to do."

The original hope was that the pain would subside with rest. A month later, however, it was clear rest wasn't helping. And on the morning of October 8, Ginyard underwent surgery that was expected to keep him out for eight weeks.

Ginyard was the one Tar Heel with an irreplaceable skill set. On a team loaded with scorers, he was the one player who relished the idea of locking down the opponent's best perimeter player. It was a reputation that began when the Alexandria, Va., native was a freshman and limited Duke sharpshooter J.J. Redick to a 5-for-21 performance on Redick's Senior Day at Cameron Indoor Stadium.

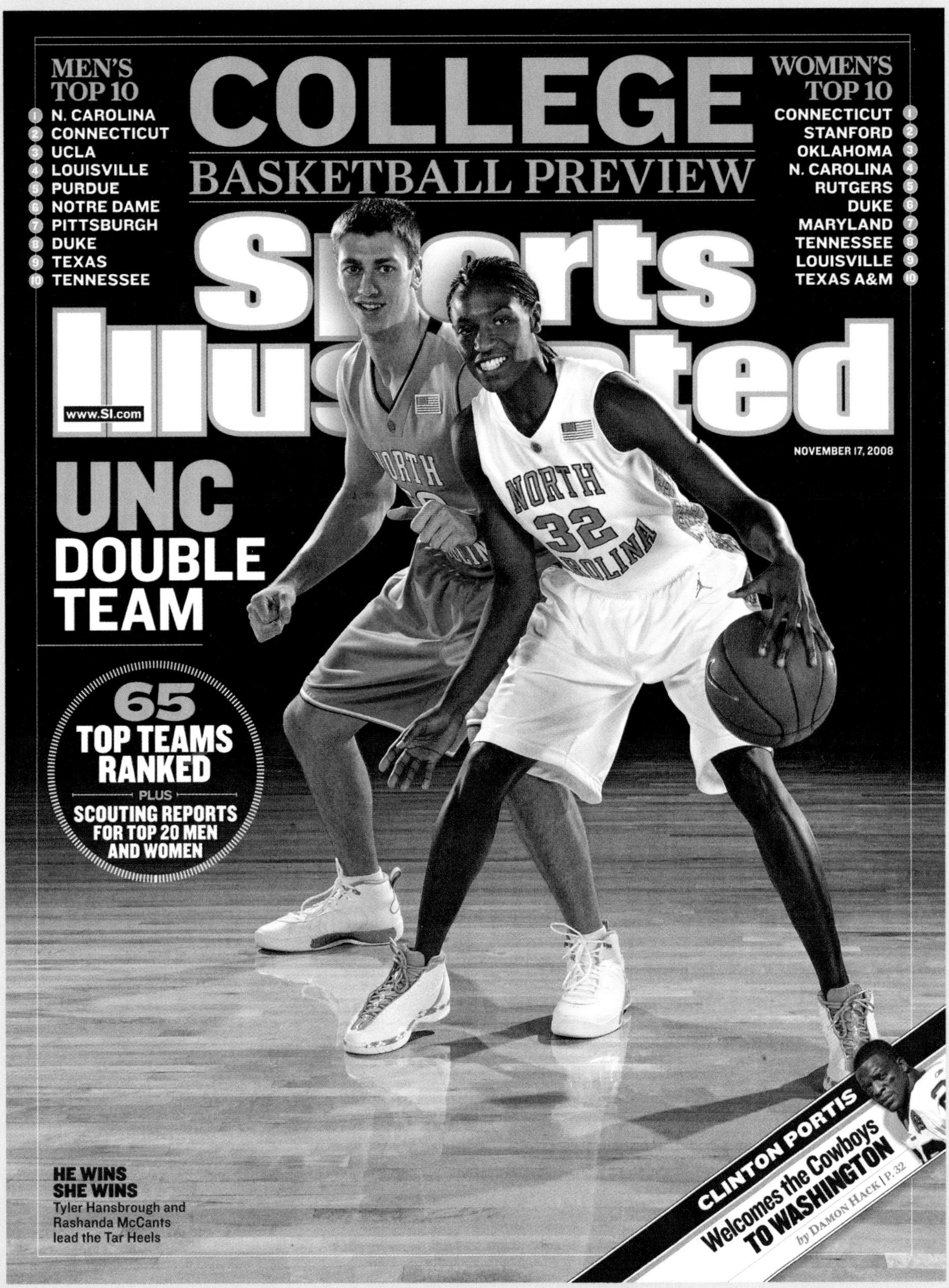

MEN'S TOP 10
1 N. CAROLINA
2 CONNECTICUT
3 UCLA
4 LOUISVILLE
5 PURDUE
6 NOTRE DAME
7 PITTSBURGH
8 DUKE
9 TEXAS
10 TENNESSEE
COLLEGE
BASKETBALL PREVIEW
WOMEN'S TOP 10
CONNECTICUT 1
STANFORD 2
OKLAHOMA 3
N. CAROLINA 4
RUTGERS 5
DUKE 6
MARYLAND 7
TENNESSEE 8
LOUISVILLE 9
TEXAS A&M 10
Sports Illustrated
www.SI.com
NOVEMBER 17, 2008
UNC
DOUBLE TEAM
65 TOP TEAMS RANKED
PLUS
SCOUTING REPORTS FOR TOP 20 MEN AND WOMEN
NORTH CAROLINA
32
HE WINS SHE WINS
Tyler Hansbrough and Rashanda McCants lead the Tar Heels
CLINTON PORTIS
Welcomes the Cowboys TO WASHINGTON
by DAMON HACK | P. 32

Marcus Ginyard had surgery on October 8, 2008. (Photo by Jim Bounds)

Ginyard had started all 39 games as a junior, but the coaching staff had already contemplated a change for the 2008–09 campaign. For three seasons, Danny Green had been the designated offensive sparkplug off the Carolina bench. Now, the coaches were considering moving him into the starting lineup.

"Before practice even started, I talked to my staff about the idea of starting Danny and having Marcus as that extra energy and hustle coming off the bench," Williams said. "I was thinking in my mind about what would be best for our team. In the past, I've always said the best defensive player should start. That's what we did in 2005, when we started Jackie Manuel.

"But at the same time, I was trying to think of what would help our team the most. Would it be Danny starting and Marcus bringing his defense off the bench, or Marcus starting and Danny bringing his offense off the bench? All of a sudden, we didn't have Marcus, so that changed everything about the process. We didn't have the option anymore."

Of course, the Carolina options were still plentiful. There was Lawson, perhaps the best point guard in the nation. There was Ellington, the perimeter marksman who had been relied upon for big shots ever since his arrival in Chapel Hill. And, of course, there was Hansbrough. There was always Hansbrough, seemingly good for 20 points and 10 rebounds even on a bad night.

Until the unthinkable happened. Two weeks before the season opener against Pennsylvania, an MRI revealed a stress reaction in Hansbrough's shin. Doctors told the senior that for the first time in his Carolina career—the first time in his basketball career, actually—he would have to scale back his workouts. He was ruled out for the season opener, the first game he would miss in his UNC career.

"When it first happened, I couldn't sleep," Hansbrough said. "I thought, 'Here's my senior year, and I'm done.' At one point I even thought, 'I should've gone to the NBA.' When someone tells me I have to relax, because of the way I work, I didn't know what to do. After two days of doing nothing, I had to do something, so I got in the pool. I can't take time off. I can't rest. Working out is what I do. And I thought the stress reaction might lead to a stress fracture and get worse."

"I'm more apprehensive than I've been in 21 years," Williams said on the day before his team opened the regular season against the Quakers. "It's really been an unsettled preseason. We spent the whole spring, summer, and fall talking about speeding up the tempo, and now we don't have the same depth."

That's how a Carolina team slated to be the first squad since the 2005 national champions to field an entire starting five of upperclassmen instead sent a true freshman, Zeller, out for the season's opening tip. And how the two leading scorers for the first game of the season—an 86–71 win over the Quakers that at one point included an on-court lineup of Drew II, Zeller, Davis, Graves, and Green—would be Zeller (18 points) and Deon Thompson (17 points).

Williams fielded the same lineup three days later against Kentucky in what has become the marquee interconference rivalry in college basketball. ESPN launched its college basketball coverage with the game, including a one-hour special leading up to the 9:00 P.M. tip-off. Noted Wildcat fan Ashley Judd was in attendance, snug in the Smith Center risers near some starstruck Tar Heel students. The movie star was a good sport about smiling for pictures, even as Carolina began to obliterate her beloved team.

They did it in a most unexpected way: with defense. Williams cagily mixed sets, alternating between a halfcourt trap, a three-quarters court trap, and man-to-man halfcourt harassment, and Ellington and Lawson completely dominated the first 10 minutes of the game by playing airtight defense. The Tar Heels raced to a 13–2 advantage in the first five minutes and 25–6 by the time Lawson hit Ellington for a rim-shaking alley-oop.

"Everyone elevated their game," Lawson said. "We started playing defense and getting into passing lanes to get steals. It was a statement to let everyone know we are here and ready to play this year."

Kentucky would finish with 28 turnovers. Caro-

Tyler Zeller had 18 points against Penn.
(Photo by Jeffrey A. Camarati)

left: Deon Thompson scored a career-high 20 points against Kentucky. (Photo by Brian Fleming)

right: Carolina players missed a combined 77 games due to injury. (Photo by Jim Bounds)

lina's offensive star was again Thompson, the junior who was thriving with Hansbrough out of the lineup. The California native had been expected to have a breakout season as a sophomore but had struggled to reach his own lofty expectations. A midseason slump sent his confidence plummeting, and he never established the type of consistency needed to be a constant force at the ACC level.

He'd also periodically mentioned his difficulties in learning to play along-side Hansbrough. Not because he had trouble sharing the spotlight, but because mechanically it was difficult for two post players to occupy the same space when one of them was as proficient as Hansbrough. Sometimes, it seemed, Thompson thought rather than reacted.

But with Hansbrough out, Thompson played more on instinct. His turn-around jumper was once again an efficient weapon. He rebounded effectively, picking up nine rebounds to go with his 20 points against Kentucky.

Thompson's role would grow even more important with less than 90 seconds remaining against the Wildcats, as Zeller was hammered on a fast break and went crashing to the floor, breaking his fall with his left hand. Doctors soon diagnosed him with a severe fracture of multiple bones in his wrist. He underwent surgery the next day.

Living with Lofty Expectations

Tyler Hansbrough, Danny Green, and the rest of the seniors knew the deal. So did Wayne Ellington and Ty Lawson. All of the players knew it. And Roy Williams most assuredly — and quite grudgingly — knew the deal as well.

What they all knew was this: practically every Tar Heel fan, college-basketball follower, and member of the media believed that a Carolina Basketball team that returned all five starters from a squad that went 36–3, won the ACC regular-season and tournament titles, and went to the Final Four needed to win a national championship for the 2008–09 season to be a success. When one of those starters is the first National Player of the Year not to turn pro since Shaquille O'Neal in 1992, and three others are former McDonald's All-Americans who deliberated for almost three months about entering the NBA Draft before also returning to college, there is only one result that will satisfy the masses.

On April 6, 2009, at Ford Field in Detroit, the largest crowd ever to watch a Final Four would either see the Tar Heels cut down the nets or watch their season end in what some would consider unqualified failure. For 366 days, since the 2008 Final Four loss to Kansas — through a historic presidential election and recession, through the annual pressure cooker that is ACC basketball — a bunch of 18-to-23-year-old college students wrestled with the notion that good was not good enough, great was not quite impressive enough, and anything short of a win on the final Monday of the season was destiny denied.

In his heart, Roy Williams knew that to be the case. But he didn't have to like it.

"It's the most unfair pressure imaginable," said the Hall of Famer, who knows a little something about the Final Four, having taken seven teams, played in the championship game four times, and won the title twice. "I was furious when we went 36–3 and somebody said the season was not a success. We won the [ACC] regular-season championship. We won the tournament championship. We went to the Final Four. Every team in the country would die for that. It will never be fair because there is so much parity, there are so many good teams."

The "experts" tabbed the Tar Heels as the logical heirs to the throne once Hansbrough, Ellington, Green, and Lawson passed on the NBA. Everyone picked Carolina number one, with the Associated Press and coaches' pre-

2008 National Player of the Year Tyler Hansbrough. (Photo by Jeffrey A. Camarati)

season polls doing so unanimously for the first time in history. Debate centered early in the season on whether they would be the game's first unbeaten champs since Indiana in 1976. Dealing with those outside expectations became part of the season's workload, just like practicing defensive slides or free throws.

"We were anointed kings of college basketball," said senior captain Bobby Frasor. "We kept telling everybody on paper, yes, we do have the best team coming back, but you don't play the game on paper."

But these Tar Heels knew how competitive the season would be and how fragile is the nature of a one-and-done tournament. They had been stung by the lopsided loss in San Antonio, but they used that disappointment to ready themselves for another run at the title.

"The way last season ended was just ridiculous," said Ellington. "To work so hard and get to the Final Four and then to forget about everything we worked for and everything we did to get there. It was a feeling that pushed us, drove us, and motivated us."

The Tar Heels also knew that the fine line between being great and being champions could be as simple as a missed box out, an unforced error, or a failure to help on defense at a key moment. These were the little things that champions do right.

"We all had one goal in mind from beginning to end," said forward Deon Thompson. "We all knew what it took; being there once showed us everything we needed to do to get back to that stage. The [Kansas] loss showed how good we *weren't* and showed us what we really needed to do to get it done."

The players believed in the notion that the individual *awards* and *rewards* go to the team that *wins* above all else. They made sacrifices to put personal goals aside to do what made the team better. You can talk about it, you can do little team-building exercises, but in the end, kids from North Carolina, Missouri, California, Pennsylvania, and other states have to believe in each other and in their coach.

"Everyone was really good friends even off the court," said senior J.B. Tanner. "There were no cliques, no one was fighting for playing time, everyone respected Coach Williams, and we had that common bond, that common goal."

Williams insists their character won through, proving once again the power of recruiting the right people.

"My team . . . put aside their dreams and goals of an NBA career and focused on the dreams and goals of the 2009 North Carolina team," said Williams. "I can't imagine that anybody could be more proud than I am of that. Never one day did those kids make us feel like they're just trying to get their own, and not one time did I ever feel those kids had anything in mind other than how our team was doing."

"It's not always being the main guy or the guy that gets all the attention," said Ellington, who was passed over in early March for all-conference honors but a scant four weeks later earned Most Outstanding Player honors at the Final Four. "It's about winning basketball games and understanding the game. That's what drove us to win a national championship."

Suddenly, the Carolina post depth that had looked overwhelming at the Late Night with Roy celebration was reduced in mid-November to just Thompson and Davis. It was a grim proposition for a club that would depart for a West Coast swing followed by a trip to Maui in less than 24 hours.

Still, as Williams made the short drive home after the Kentucky game— he didn't have official word on Zeller yet, but he knew it was unlikely to be positive—he considered all the adversity his team had faced in the first week of the season. Then he replayed the critical plays of that night's shellacking of the Wildcats, one of the most prestigious programs in the nation and a team that boasted two eventual members of the All-SEC squad.

"To see that kind of performance, especially on the defensive end, was impressive," the head coach said. "And to see that kind of result without Tyler, and with Deon and Ed stepping up and the perimeter guys doing the job, was impressive. I went home that night thinking, 'Well, that should have really told this team something.'"

What would happen over the next seven days in California and Maui would tell them even more. Just like the 2005 national championship team, the Tar Heels were about to use a Hawaiian vacation to make their first definitive statement of their candidacy for a national title.

Trips with Purpose

It has become commonplace for East Coast teams making the journey to the Maui Invitational to stop on the way out to the islands and play a game on the West Coast. It breaks up an extremely long trip, lets players get adjusted to the time change more gradually, and allows a team to squeeze more games out of the trip.

But Roy Williams doesn't believe in playing just any games. He wants to play games that will help his team later in the season.

That's how Carolina ended up at the Thunderdome on the campus of UC Santa Barbara. The Gauchos were a good team with a veteran coach—attributes Williams considers important in finding an opponent. But their home arena was equally important.

Since returning to Carolina, Williams had built the Tar Heels into a formidable road program. He did it in a way that's still foreign to many of his contemporaries at elite programs: by going on the road and playing in hostile environments, even when such a game isn't a requirement. Carolina could have played a neutral-site game at the Staples Center or the Pond in Anaheim. Any of the area's numerous Division I colleges would have been excited just to get a game against the Tar Heels, no matter the location. But Williams wanted a road game. And not just any road game, but a tough road game.

An ESPN program manager who makes many of the network's broadcast choices—often based on the environment presented by the home crowd—once said: "If I had to pick the three best places in the nation in terms of noise and enthusiasm, they would be Duke, UCSB, and Rutgers."

Not coincidentally, Carolina voluntarily played at both Rutgers and UCSB during the careers of the senior class. The Tar Heels also won in both of those venues, a fitting tune-up for ACC competition.

"It's huge that we have the opportunity to play the Tar Heels, period, but to play them at home is even more special," said UCSB head coach Bob Williams.

"This is definitely a major game of interest for the program and the community."

In fact, it was the first time a top-ranked team had come to UCSB since Jerry Tarkanian brought his impressive 1991 UNLV squad for what was then a conference game. Tarkanian left suitably impressed: "I don't believe there's anyplace in the country better than this," he said.

Williams consistently makes an effort to ensure his teams do more than just play a basketball game when playing road games. The head coach is aware that some of his players are traveling extensively for the first time when they become Tar Heels, so it's not unusual for a lengthy road trip to include a taste of the area. In Memphis, Carolina would tour the Civil Rights Museum and eat at Rendezvous, a nationally known barbeque fixture. When visiting Washington, D.C., for a postseason visit with President Barack Obama, the team bus also drove by several of the famous monuments.

And in California for the game at UCSB, the Tar Heels received a special invitation from Los Angeles resident Gary Cypres to tour his personal sports-memorabilia collection, an assortment widely considered one of the best in the world and soon to be part of the Sports Museum of Los Angeles. Cypres's haul, which he amassed with a fortune made in investment banking, includes the original cornerstone from Yankee Stadium, one of the famous T206 Honus Wagner baseball cards, a Heisman Trophy, and numerous other items that filled an estimated 32,000 square feet.

"It was unbelievable," said Marcus Ginyard. "The guy had stuff that you've only heard about or seen in movies."

Eventually, though, it was time for basketball. Williams and his players were greeted by a boisterous Thunderdome student section, which encompassed the entire sideline across from the benches and much of the end zones. The low wooden roof held in the noise, making it an environment similar to Carmichael Auditorium, where a crowd of several thousand could sound like many more because of the acoustics. The capacity crowd of 6,000 behaved the way Williams wanted; they were extremely hostile, just as the Tar Heels would experience in later ACC games. In fact, the Gauchos possessed the best mascot Carolina would see all year: a student known as "The Phantom," who spent most of his time beneath the bleachers but would, when a time-out was called, sprint onto the court to lead the sellout crowd in high school–type shout alongs. His favorite included spelling out U-C-S-B with his body, occasionally asking the crowd to shout "U" and whisper "C," then shout "S" and whisper "B."

But for the first time this season, the Tar Heels suited up something even more powerful than The Phantom: Tyler Hansbrough. After missing two games, the big man returned to the starting lineup against the Gauchos. He wasn't completely himself, shooting just 2-for-8 from the field after suffering a sprained ankle less than two minutes into the game while absorbing some contact on a layup. He still experienced pain in his shin after the game. But he also made 10 trips to the free-throw line, converting nine, and grabbed seven rebounds.

UCSB grabbed an early 27–22 lead to stoke the sellout crowd, but Ty Lawson responded with back-to-back three-pointers and then sprawled on the floor to try and corral a loose ball.

Lawson would finish with a team-high 19 points in the 84–67 victory, gaining the respect of Gaucho guard Paul Roemer, who had the unenviable task of trying to defend him for most of the night.

"That guy," Roemer said. "You think you're in exactly the right position in front of him, and somehow he goes by you."

After the game, the Tar Heels packed their belongings onto a charter bus and made the 99-mile drive to a hotel near the Los Angeles airport. An early-morning flight to Maui awaited.

ROY WILLIAMS LOVES a few things. He loves his family, of course, and a good round of golf. Sometimes he even loves a bad round of golf.

And then there's Maui. Williams really, really loves Maui. Before the coach's return to Chapel Hill, the Tar Heels had played in the Maui Invitational once in the previous eight seasons. Since then, they've played twice in the past five seasons and are already slated to return for the 2012 event. NCAA rules permit a team to appear in Maui once every four seasons, and the Tar Heels plan to do exactly that.

"As long as I'm here," Williams said, "we're going to play in Maui as much as we can."

The reasons are numerous. First, Maui is one of the world's great vacation destinations. The weather is usually very good; when the Tar Heels landed, there was a rain shower that lasted less than three hours, and the apologetic locals acted as if a catastrophic typhoon had hit the island. There's plenty for the players to do within walking distance of the hotel, and it's a destination most of them have never been to before. The event is professionally organized and exceptionally well run, with none of the extra hassles that Williams despises.

And, of course, for all of the above reasons, the Maui Invitational annually collects the most competitive field of any of the preseason tournaments. A powerhouse team like the Tar Heels can expect a fairly easy first-round game, but the next two contests are likely to be against NCAA Tournament–caliber competition.

The only negative aspect of the Maui trip is the extraordinarily long flight required to get there. Fortunately, the Tar Heels flew nonstop from Los Angeles to Maui and received an extra bonus when they encountered rapper Soulja Boy outside Gate 48A at the Los Angeles Airport. Players were sprawled across the uncomfortable waiting area chairs when Hansbrough nudged Lawson.

"Hey," Hansbrough said, "there's your guy."

"Huh?" the still-sleepy Lawson replied.

"It's Soulja Boy," said Hansbrough, whose chances of identifying the rapper as an incoming freshman would have been very slim. Lawson, Will Graves, and several other Tar Heels took time to chat with the music star, who was sporting a platinum chain that was so large it might have counted as his carry-on bag.

Upon arriving in Maui, the team had just a few hours before the first scheduled off-court event, in which Mike Copeland dispatched all challengers—including Lawson, his competition in the championship round—to win a video-game contest among players from the eight participating teams.

Marc Campbell in Maui.
(Photo by Jim Hawkins)

That a Tar Heel would win the video-game contest was no surprise, as Rashad McCants had won it during the 2004 event. Most of Copeland and Lawson's teammates crowded around the screens to offer dubious advice.

The implications of his team putting two players in the finals of a video-game contest weren't lost on Williams.

"Mike Copeland should have won," he said. "With his ACL surgery, he hasn't practiced one day. It sort of bothered me that he beat Ty Lawson, because he's one who was supposed to be practicing basketball."

Two days later, the Tar Heels finally hit the court against host Chaminade, a Division II team most famous for upsetting Virginia in 1982. The Silverswords didn't quite have the same upset potential in 2008, so Joe Holladay approached J.B. Tanner, a senior from Hendersonville, N.C., before the game and said the words that every walk-on loves to hear: "You're good for five minutes tonight."

"Really?" Tanner asked excitedly.

"Easily," Holladay said.

Tanner then proceeded to drain 19 straight three-pointers during warm-ups—good practice for his six minutes of game action, during which he scored nine points in the 115–70 rout.

"We got a lot of playing time in that game," Tanner said of himself and his fellow walk-ons. "It reminded me of going back to the JV days. It was a lot of fun being able to score some points and seeing the other guys on the Blue Team do well."

In the semifinal round against Oregon, a similar situation occurred. Jerod Haase approached Patrick Moody, a walk-on from Asheville, before the game.

"Today is your day, Moody," Haase said. Once again, the Tar Heel coaching staff proved prescient, as Moody scored six points in four minutes in a Carolina victory highlighted by the return (again) of Hansbrough, who had sat out the Chaminade win with a sprained ankle.

Williams had debated the wisdom of playing his senior star in back-to-back games, which put Hansbrough's availability for the championship game against Notre Dame in question.

At least, everyone other than Hansbrough questioned it. He wanted to play no matter what. This was an eighth-ranked Notre Dame team that featured Luke Harangody, a standout power forward who some observers considered to be Hansbrough's equal. Hansbrough makes a point of saying he doesn't watch much college basketball, but he was well aware of Harangody—his teammates had made sure of that.

"I liked to call Harangody the 'bootleg Tyler,'" Deon Thompson said with a grin. Bobby Frasor—who would frequently trade barbs with Hansbrough in practice to the point that the good friends would later have to offer brusque apologies to each other at the house they shared off campus—was equally merciless.

"There have been comparisons of Harangody and me ever since last year," Hansbrough said. "Some of my teammates called me 'Hansgody' because they knew it made me mad, and that was something I wanted to end right there. I wanted to play against him and knock them out and take care of business."

But even 15 minutes before tip-off, Hansbrough's availability wasn't a certainty. Williams approached him during pregame warm-ups to inquire about his status.

"Hey Tyler," the coach said, "how are you—"

"Fine," Hansbrough interrupted brusquely. "I'm fine."

Keeping him out of the game could have resulted in physical harm to Williams. Over the previous four days, Hansbrough had grown increasingly irritable. He had emerged from his hotel room only rarely. Before the Oregon game, Frasor knocked on Hansbrough's door.

"Want to get some breakfast?" he asked harmlessly.

"No," Hansbrough coldly replied. "I got room service and ate by myself."

Frasor would later advise C.B. McGrath that it might be wise to post a guard at Hansbrough's balcony to prevent the big man from throwing himself into the Pacific Ocean in frustration. Later that day, at the team's pregame meal, Frasor tried again to communicate.

"Hey," he said to Hansbrough, "did you do anything today?"

"No," Hansbrough replied.

And that was it. No elaboration. No attempt at conversation. No polite chatter. Just "no."

"Oh, okay," Frasor said. "I didn't do anything, either. Thanks for asking."

So Williams was lucky he didn't draw back a nub after daring to ask Hansbrough if he might want to play against the Fighting Irish. Of course he was playing. Of course he was starting. And, given his history, of course he would shoot 13-of-19 from the field to total a team-high 34 points in a complete annihilation of Notre Dame. Harangody, who played despite having a virus, finished with 13 points. More notably, Harangody was the victim of a

J.B. Tanner scored a career-high nine points versus Chaminade. (Photo by J. D. Lyon Jr.)

vicious one-handed dunk by Thompson, who contributed 19 points and 13 rebounds.

Hansbrough hit jumpers, made post moves, and tossed in a three-pointer. He grabbed five rebounds and blocked two shots. In other words, he did all the things a National Player of the Year is supposed to do, including win the game by a 102–87 final margin that was deceivingly close thanks to the phenomenal late-game shooting of Notre Dame's Kyle McAlarney.

While Hansbrough was reverting to old form, Ty Lawson was earning MVP honors with a 22-point, 11-assist performance that evoked memories of Raymond Felton's MVP effort in 2004.

"I made a statement tonight," Hansbrough said on the Maui Civic Center court immediately after the game.

"That was one of my best games in college," Hansbrough said. "People were doubting me and I took a lot of criticism. I couldn't turn on ESPN without people saying, 'He's not the Tyler Hansbrough he used to be.' I wanted to prove I was back."

Back, too, were the Tar Heels, claiming the program's third Maui championship and second in the past five seasons. But there was still some drama remaining before the team could leave the islands.

Ty Lawson was MVP of the Maui Invitational. (Photo by J. D. Lyon Jr.)

ALTHOUGH THE HEAD COACH himself has never jumped, Williams-coached teams in Maui have made a tradition of cliff-jumping off Black Rock, known to the natives as Pu'u Keka'a.

Even the Carolina freshmen experienced the leap—after some goading.

"Ed told me he wasn't going to jump off the cliff unless I did," Larry Drew II said. "I told him it was nothing for me to do it. I wanted to see his 6-foot-10 body fall off that cliff."

"I cut my foot going up there," Davis said of the sharp rock. "Larry did it, so I did it too. He was telling me I was too scared, so I had to climb up there."

Indeed, the ascension to the peak was probably more treacherous than the actual jump. Several Notre Dame players on hand at virtually the same time decided not to risk the rocky climb, and they were joined on the sidelines by Thompson. He did participate in a team snorkeling excursion, however, when all the Tar Heels strapped on fins and goggles and went trolling for sea life.

As it turned out, however, Thompson did not waver when he and his teammates were faced with a much more serious situation. The team flew back on American Airlines Flight 6 from Maui, a flight that left on Thanksgiving night. Just as the plane began to roll back from the gate, flight attendant Penny Mather streaked up the left aisle of the Boeing 763 and shouted, "Code red!"

A large man who had come on board in a wheelchair was struggling. Sweat was pouring off him and his family couldn't get him to respond. He had a history of diabetes and heart problems.

"I need strong guys!" Mather barked.

Video coordinator Eric Hoots, Hansbrough, and Thompson jumped to their feet. Mather grabbed the automatic external defibrillator that is kept on board. "We need to pick him up," she said.

left: Wayne Ellington went snorkeling in Hawaii.
(Photo by J. D. Lyon Jr.)

right: Ed Davis cleared Black Rock in Maui.
(Photo by J. D. Lyon Jr.)

Thompson, Hansbrough, and Hoots lifted the man to a seven-footer's height. "Not that high!" Mather said, having forgotten that she was dealing with larger-than-normal humans.

The Tar Heels took the man to the galley, where two doctors on board could attend to him. After about 30 minutes, he was restored to consciousness enough to wheel him off the plane. Passengers gave Mather a round of applause as she walked down the aisle, the first time that has happened to her in her 20 years of flying.

The heroes of the day, she insisted, were the players.

"That's a great group you're with," she told a member of the Tar Heel traveling party.

Winning the Recruiting Game

The 2008–09 Carolina Basketball season kicked off for the public with the Late Night with Roy Williams ceremonies on October 24, 2008. For some team members, stung by the way the previous campaign had ended, the season might have begun six months earlier, as soon as the final seconds of the loss to Kansas ticked off the clock at the 2008 Final Four in San Antonio.

In reality, though, the ride to the 2009 national championship began a full four years before Wayne Ellington, Tyler Hansbrough, and their cohorts led the Tar Heels to the title-game victory over Michigan State in Detroit.

Less than 48 hours after Carolina won the 2005 NCAA title, Roy Williams hit the road for the tiny mountain town of Mouth of Wilson, Va., home to the famed Oak Hill Academy and its then-junior point guard, Ty Lawson.

Recruiting is the lifeblood of any successful college basketball program, even one coming off a national championship. Carolina is no different, and Williams needed a point guard with the pending departure of Raymond Felton for the NBA Draft lottery. Lawson was impressed that Williams, rather than basking in the glow of the NCAA title, chose to come to a town miles from the middle of nowhere to speak to him.

Some of the pieces of the 2009 championship puzzle were already in place before Williams visited Lawson, of course. Hansbrough, Bobby Frasor, Marcus Ginyard, Danny Green, and Mike Copeland, the class that Williams called a "nucleus group," would enroll in summer school at UNC that June and help Carolina to an unexpectedly successful season as freshmen in 2005–06.

"I think you could say that [class] worked out pretty well," Williams deadpanned.

Frasor and Hansbrough both attended the 2005 championship game win over Illinois, sitting in the Carolina section of the Edward Jones Dome in St. Louis. Hansbrough, the biggest prize in the 2005–06 UNC freshman class, came close to not wearing Carolina Blue because of a miserable recruiting trip to Chapel Hill months earlier. An ice storm during his official visit stranded Hansbrough in Chapel Hill for an extra night when all he wanted to do was go home and focus on which college he would attend.

"When I first came to Chapel Hill, it's kind of funny because I actually hated the university and didn't really like anything about it," Hansbrough said.

Even Williams thought he had no chance to land the big man from the small town of Poplar Bluff, Missouri.

"We take him to the airport and the flight is postponed, the flight is canceled and we bring him back to my house," Williams said. "We're out there scraping ice off of my car to get him back to the room so he can sleep. He's going to have to stay another night and not go back until the next day. When he left, I said, 'We're not going to get that kid.'"

Hansbrough's father, Gene, who had developed a close relationship with Williams, assistant Joe Holladay, and the rest of the UNC coaching staff, encouraged Tyler to keep an open mind. Over time, and after another visit to Chapel Hill during warmer weather, the younger Hansbrough was convinced. He never regretted his decision for a minute.

More heated recruiting battles and hard work by Williams and his staff eventually brought the rest of the 2008–09 Tar Heel team together.

Ellington might have attended hometown Villanova had Holladay not made a late detour to Philadelphia to see Episcopal Academy teammates Ellington and Gerald Henderson during a scouting trip to Delaware.

"I heard about a couple of kids at this private school from a friend of mine, so I flew up early that morning, and I called the coach, and he said they were going to have a shootaround," said Holladay. "So I went into this gym at Episcopal. For about an hour, I watched them just shoot. I walked outside the door and called Coach Williams and said, 'Hey, there's two kids here we're going to offer—we'll offer scholarships.'"

Williams agreed. "It was a question of getting him away from home, but I think he liked everything we were saying," he said of Ellington. "I said, 'Son, we need someone that can score. Rashad McCants is going to be gone.'"

Tyler Hansbrough and his dad, Gene, on Senior Day. (Photo by Robert Crawford)

Ellington chose to leave home and head south for Chapel Hill. His classmate, Deon Thompson from California, nearly attended Gonzaga, the West Coast school Carolina would eventually defeat in the 2009 Sweet 16 in Memphis.

"Mark Few had a big effect on my mother, and their whole staff did a great job recruiting me," Thompson said of the Gonzaga coach. "I could have been a Zag, but I am proud to be a Tar Heel. The biggest reason I came here was Coach Williams and how real of a person he is and how respected he is.

"He is absolutely what he was when he came in my house to recruit me," continued Thompson. "He came into my house by himself and he is still the same person today. That is something a lot of kids should pray for when going through recruiting. Guys can come into your home and tell you how much they care about you, and then when you get to school, they forget your name. I got lucky for someone to come into my house who is a great person, a great man, and still the same person today."

Freshman Ed Davis signed on with the Tar Heels mainly because of Williams's demonstrated ability to develop big men into solid players. Davis's father, Terry, played 10 years in the professional ranks.

"Ed's father was an NBA player, liked the way we played, and felt like it would be good for his son," Williams said.

Hard recruiting work also helped sway Tyler Zeller, another prep All-American big man, to spurn schools in his home state of Indiana for Carolina.

"I made more trips personally to Washington [Zeller's hometown] than any other head coach," Williams said. "I think that might have shown him how confident I was that he could really be a good player for us."

Winning a second national championship just four years after the 2005 title with an entirely rebuilt team demonstrates impressive work by Williams and his staff. Not being one to fall behind, Williams was back on the road recruiting again just a few days after beating Michigan State, trying to find the next batch of NCAA champions to wear Carolina Blue.

Freshman Tyler Zeller. (Photo by Jeffrey A. Camarati)

CHAPTER THREE

"They're Dead"

"Criticism is something you can avoid easily by saying nothing, doing nothing, and being nothing."

Thought for the Day, December 2, 2008

Carolina had just waxed UNC Asheville, 116–48, at the Smith Center. It was the third-largest margin of victory in Carolina history and the most points by the Tar Heels in Roy Williams's six-year UNC head-coaching career.

Marc Campbell and Danny Green were not concerned about those stats. Campbell, a junior guard and the son of a Tar Heel letterman, had just watched Green toss in six second-half three-pointers. On the way back to the locker room after the rout, the team was still buzzing about Green's performance, the most three-pointers by a Tar Heel in three years.

"That looked like Tayshaun," Campbell said. He was referring to Tayshaun Prince's three-point explosion against the Tar Heels in 2001, when the Kentucky sharpshooter nailed five straight three-pointers in the first four minutes of a game in Lexington. The last was a straightaway trifecta from the edge of the Kentucky logo, just like Green's final three-pointer had been from the edge of the outline of the state of North Carolina on the Smith Center floor.

That shot was one Green described as a "heat check"—a fling just to find out exactly how hot he was. The answer: smoking.

"When I looked at the video board afterwards, I was like, 'Wow, that was pretty far,'" Green said. "I'm lucky I made it, because if I had missed it, I'm sure Coach would have been a little upset."

"Did Prince hit his all in a row?" Bobby Frasor asked as the Tar Heels shuffled to the locker room. This turned into a major point of contention among the players, with Campbell eventually going to the ultimate source: YouTube.

While his teammates were debating exactly where Green's explosion ranked on the all-time list of hot streaks, Green himself was blissfully unaware.

"I never saw that Kentucky-Carolina game," he said. "Did Tayshaun get really hot in that game?"

Almost as hot as you were today, he was told.

"I might have to get a tape of that one," Green said with a grin.

NO ONE EXPECTED THE STREAK of blowouts to continue into the next game, when the Tar Heels had to travel to Detroit for a made-for-TV matchup against 12th-ranked Michigan State at Ford Field, the site of the 2009 Final Four. The game was part of the ACC–Big Ten Challenge, but it was also being billed as a possible Final Four preview.

With the game came all of the trappings of a post-season showdown: big venue, big crowd, big distance from the locker room to the court. A Tar Heel assistant was dispatched to determine how long it would take the players and coaches to get from their locker room to the playing surface. It turned out to be nearly a three-minute hike, which was approximately the same amount of time it took Carolina to take control of the game.

Ty Lawson had been the recipient of some indirect trash talk from Spartan sophomore point guard Kalin Lucas. Through a mutual acquaintance, Lucas had proclaimed he was planning to score at least 20 points on Lawson. Instead, Lucas shot 2-for-10, while Lawson posted 17 points, eight assists, seven steals, and zero turnovers.

"I wanted to show him how good I was," Lawson said. "I like it when people talk trash, because it brings out another level of competitiveness in me. We wanted to come out and make a statement. It was a top-ten team and it was at Ford Field, so we wanted to have a good showing. We came out real strong and played very well in that game."

With 6:31 remaining in the first half, Carolina held just a 33–29 lead. But they stretched that advantage to 14 points by halftime and then crushed the Spartans with an overwhelming second-half blitzkrieg.

MSU was without big man Goran Suton and had played three games in Orlando the previous week-

Danny Green sank six three-pointers against UNC Asheville. (Photo by Brian Fleming)

left: Ty Lawson had 17 points and seven steals in the ACC–Big 10 Challenge. (Photo by Jim Hawkins)

right: Carolina blasted the Spartans by 35 in their first meeting. (Photo by Jim Hawkins)

opposite: Tyler Hansbrough had 25 points and 11 boards in the 98–63 win. (Photo by Jim Hawkins)

end, a hectic travel schedule Roy Williams noted in his postgame comments. Of course, his team had just come off a four-games-in-six-days whirlwind through California and Maui.

"I thought that game was going down to the wire," Williams said. "But right before the half, I said, 'They're dead.' I knew we had an extra day's rest over them, and I knew our physical conditioning was much better than theirs and that extra day of rest was important. Right before half, I said, 'They're done. If we keep the hammer down, this one is going to be over early in the second half.'"

Keeping the hammer down hadn't always been a Carolina strength, as the talented Tar Heels sometimes lost interest in the second half of blowouts. This time, however, Williams focused on maintaining their intensity.

With a 30-point lead midway through the second half, he was still begging his team for tough defense. With less than nine minutes left, the head coach approached Danny Green, Bobby Frasor, Ed Davis, and Larry Drew II at the scorer's table, where they were preparing to check into the game. The Tar Heel advantage was 29 points.

"I don't want anything sloppy out there," Williams said.

In the afterglow of the 35-point win—the second-worst defeat in Tom Izzo's decorated career in East Lansing—Frasor said, "It's fun when you see the lead is at 30 or 35, and we'll say, 'Let's get it to 40.' It's the end of the game and you're still excited because you're still trying to reach some goals."

To that point in the season, Ford Field's primary tenant, the Detroit Lions, had scored 93 points in six home games (360 minutes of action). It took the Tar Heels just one 40-minute game to post 98 points.

That kind of offensive explosion immediately prompted chatter about a return trip to Detroit in April. Even the players weren't immune to speculating about the implications of the blowout.

"That was just crazy," said senior Jack Wooten, a Burlington native. "The walk-ons got three minutes against a top-10 team and we almost scored 100 points. I definitely read some articles saying Carolina had punched their ticket back to Detroit already. That was a ridiculous statement because so much can happen. But the way we played there . . . we knew we had a chance to get back if we played the way we had been. We knew it was a realistic possibility."

Patrick Moody, one of seven UNC players from the Tar Heel State. (Photo by J. D. Lyon Jr.)

opposite: The Tar Heels trailed only one time in the December matchup. (Photo by Jim Hawkins)

Lawson Takes Control

It was late on the night of December 3, 2008, and Carolina had just trounced Michigan State by 35 points in Detroit in the ACC–Big Ten Challenge, but a loud argument was in progress in the otherwise smug Tar Heel locker room.

Ty Lawson had just amassed 17 points, eight assists, and seven steals without a turnover against the Spartans in a mere 28 minutes. The brilliant effort boosted his assist/turnover ratio to 6.11 (55 assists against just nine turnovers in eight games).

"Really, I can do it," Lawson argued. "At least I'm going to try to keep it going as long as I can. It might not end up at 7 to 1 for the whole season, but it'll be good, I promise you that."

"No way," countered Lawson's roommate and reserve point guard Marc Campbell. "Nobody can keep that up for a whole season!"

Four months later, in a locker room in the same building, Lawson was celebrating another win over the Spartans. He had been dazzling on both ends of the floor once again, pilfering an NCAA championship-game record eight steals and tallying 21 points, six assists, and one turnover while hitting 15 of 18 free-throw attempts.

Lawson's pair of strong efforts against MSU were among a multitude of impressive individual statistical achievements in 2008–09.

Tyler Hansbrough became the leading scorer in Carolina and ACC history, made more free throws than any player in NCAA annals, and broke a plethora of other records. Danny Green ended his career with more wins and games played than any other Tar Heel.

The team posted impressive numbers as well.

Carolina's seniors went 124–22 in their four seasons, the most wins of any class in UNC history. The national title win in Detroit ended a two-year stretch during which the Tar Heels won 42 of 46 games played away from the Smith Center.

For the year, Carolina led the nation in average margin of victory and was second in scoring. The team's average margin of victory was 20.2 points per game in the NCAA Tournament, the highest since Indiana blitzed the field in 1981.

Clearly, the Tar Heels had plenty of gaudy statistics in 2008–09 — after all, teams don't win national championships without dominating performances along the way.

For all that Carolina accomplished statistically in winning its fifth NCAA championship, however, Lawson's spectacular assist/turnover ratio of 3.49, the best in ACC history, stands alone.

"When Ty wants to play," said Hansbrough, "he's one of those players—when he turns it on and plays, you can't do much about it."

Lawson's mastery of Roy Williams's offense, his ability to get the ball to the right man at the right spot on the floor without turning it over—all while playing at breakneck speed—made the Tar Heels nearly impossible to beat unless they shot poorly.

It also garnered Lawson ACC Player of the Year honors and the Cousy Award as the nation's top point guard.

From an easy December win over Michigan State to another victory on the same court against the same opponent four months later, Lawson relentlessly steered the Carolina attack.

"His decision making was better," said Williams. "He didn't make plays too early and he didn't make plays too late. Ty has always been a ball-possession guard who plays at a very fast tempo, which is extremely hard. I have never seen a guard at that fast a tempo have anywhere close to that assist/error ratio."

Lawson always took good care of the ball, posting an assist/turnover ratio of 2.57 as a freshman and 2.36 during an injury-limited sophomore campaign. But he shined brightest as a junior, particularly in the NCAA Tournament, during which he averaged almost 21 points while amassing 34 assists against just seven turnovers (a ratio of 4.86).

"I can't imagine any point guard playing any better the last four games in the NCAA Tournament since Isiah Thomas in 1981," Williams said. "It was at a different level."

It took time for Lawson to master the delicate

Ty Lawson became the first point guard in history to lead the Tar Heels in field-goal percentage. (Photo by Jeffrey A. Camarati)

Lawson won the Cousy Award as the nation's top point guard. (Photo by Jack Morton)

balance of when to pass and when to shoot in Williams's offense, sometimes prompting the coach to urge him to shoot the ball more often.

"I learned over the years," Lawson said. "My freshman year, I used to drive so deep in the lane I had nowhere to pass the ball. This year, before I made any moves with the ball, I tried to see what would happen—if I could get in the lane, if there was help on defense. It was just something you have to learn over the years to be in control but still play fast."

The Carolina coaches relished the new-and-improved Lawson. Assistant coach C.B. McGrath noted that Lawson became so confident that he felt unguardable at times.

"I have always told Ty to manage the game," said fellow assistant Steve Robinson. "I never really tried to define what 'manage the game' was. It was not turning the basketball over in my mind. It's keep charging, keep attacking, making plays, getting the basketball to the guy who's hot. He just understood."

Lawson was so steady offensively and so improved defensively that he had more steals than turnovers on the season—a rare feat.

"He sensed that he was playing at a different level than he had played before, and his leadership qualities were at a different level than he had showed before," said Williams, who also called Lawson "the engine that drove the car" all season.

"His assist-to-turnover ratio, his field-goal percentage, his free-throw percentage, his steals—everything that a point guard should do—he did and went beyond that," said Bobby Frasor. "It was an amazing run."

Dog Days

The *Old Farmer's Almanac* lists the traditional timing of the dog days as the 40 days beginning July 3 and ending August 11. In the farming world, or the baseball world, or any part of the world not centered on a 94-by-50 piece of hardwood, that might be true.

In college basketball, the dog days begin in December.

"At that point, right at the end of the nonconference schedule when you have exams, that's a little bit of the dog days of the basketball season," Roy Williams said. "I always try to fight through it because I don't like [that feeling], but it's just the fact of the matter."

It's about as close as the Carolina head coach will ever come to admitting that sometimes during the basketball season, life gets in the way of hoops. Players are dealing with exams—always challenging, but especially thorny this year with the amount of class time that they missed traveling to Maui and Detroit. Holiday hustle and bustle saps even the rowdiest crowds of their energy. The long-awaited marquee nonconference games are over, but the eagerly anticipated league games are still several weeks away.

That's how unremarkable games like a 100–84 victory over Oral Roberts end up on the schedule. After Carolina took a 10-day layoff for exams, the Golden Eagles actually outscored the Tar Heels, 50–46, in the second half.

"We were not sharp at all," Williams said. "We were not good defensively. I was not pleased at all with what we did on the backboards or on the defensive end."

The defensive shortcomings immediately gave the head coach something to focus on in practice. But he also had to acknowledge the buzz around Tyler Hansbrough, who was just nine points away from breaking Phil Ford's all-time UNC scoring record. Ford's mark had stood for 30 years, and there had already been significant discussion about how to best honor the achievement. Thanks to Hansbrough's early-season injuries, the momentous game would

left: Tyler Hansbrough broke Phil Ford's UNC scoring record against Evansville. (Photo by J. D. Lyon Jr.)

right: Carolina legends Phil Ford and Tyler Hansbrough. (Photo by Jeffrey A. Camarati)

come at the Smith Center, where plans were made to briefly halt the game and acknowledge the senior's achievement.

Williams addressed his team about the imminent occasion at practice the day before. In the team huddle before they broke into groups for drills, Williams said, "We need to play our tails off. Let's get this record for Tyler, and then let's get on with it."

Then he looked at Hansbrough. "Tyler, I know you're going to be focused on

A Senior Leader's Bittersweet Season

Roy Williams knows a good hug when he gets one. There was that memorable bear hug in 2005 with Sean May after the Tar Heels beat Illinois for the championship. There are the heartfelt ones with seniors each year at the final home game. And in Detroit, there were triumphant ones with Tyler Hansbrough, Ty Lawson, and the other starters near the one-minute mark of the championship game win over Michigan State. Hugs and tears are no strangers to the coach.

But there was one hug Williams couldn't bear to give that April night, so he turned and went the other way. When the buzzer sounded and the Tar Heels rushed the floor, there was just no way Williams was prepared to handle the outpouring of emotions that would come with embracing Marcus Ginyard, his 21-year-old team leader who missed all but three games due to injury.

The senior from Alexandria, Va., started all 39 games in 2007–08, earned All-ACC Tournament, ACC All-Defensive Team, and Carolina's defensive-player-of-the-year honors. But early last summer, his left foot began to ache, then he sprained his ankle in August, exacerbating a developing stress fracture. He underwent surgery to piece his fifth metatarsal back together in October.

The Tar Heels were now without their emotional beacon, their best perimeter defender, and one of their most explosive offensive rebounders. Worse for Ginyard, his nightmare season was just beginning. Thus began the four-month-long drama of whether he would or would not play again that year.

"For a long time I didn't know whether I should listen to my head or my heart," said Ginyard. "I just wanted to get out there and play to the point where sometimes I was telling myself that my foot didn't hurt just to come to find out it was killing me and I probably shouldn't have been doing some of the things I was doing."

At first, doctors thought he would be back by early to mid-December. But by Christmas, Ginyard had not played, and he even regressed over the holiday break. But he had to give playing a shot, so on December 28th he made his return against Rutgers. He played 11 minutes and scored three points. Over the next two games, he played 26 more minutes and added just one more free throw.

Then he shut it down. He had to, because someone was wearing his familiar number 1 jersey, but it wasn't the Marcus Ginyard we'd seen for three previous seasons. He wasn't able to cut and drive the ball from the wing, he wasn't

able to attack the glass, and he wasn't able to apply the lockdown defensive effort that had become his calling card.

"I was battling more against my foot than I was the other team," said Ginyard. "You're not going to be able to compete and perform at the level you're used to when the first thought is how your foot's moving or how your foot's feeling. It wasn't ready and I wasn't going to be able to do the things we had planned and I wanted to do."

So in early January, he sat out again, and on February 3 he announced he would miss the rest of the season, ending his dream of playing alongside his housemates Hansbrough, Bobby Frasor, and Danny Green in their quest for a national championship.

"It was extremely difficult for me to tell my senior classmates," recalled Ginyard. "Those relationships are the very center of my best memories of college basketball and playing here at Carolina. Not being able to finish out my senior year with those guys was one of the most difficult things about making the decision to redshirt. But those relationships are something I'm going to cherish for the rest of my life."

Senior Day is always an emotional cauldron for those playing their final home game, but for Ginyard it emphasized a stark reality that his class would be moving on without him. Seven seniors, not eight, were feted that day, but Frasor interrupted the proceedings to invite Ginyard to join them at midcourt.

"Marcus is definitely class of '09," said Frasor, who lived with Ginyard for three seasons. "I don't care what year his diploma says or what year he does graduate. He came in with us. He's always going to be remembered as part of our class."

Williams put Ginyard on the bench for all six games in the NCAA Tournament, selecting an active player to sit in the stands each game to stay within prescribed roster limits.

"That meant the world to me," said Ginyard. "There are no words to describe the feeling you have with your teammates when we were able to do the things we did. To be right there and to be so involved, I just couldn't see it happening any other way."

Even in a suit, Ginyard made an impact on the title run.

"What was amazing was how he was able to really lead," said senior Patrick Moody. "He would encourage us before games and would be in the huddles talking and pumping us up. Right before we went on the floor [for the championship game], he said, 'We've worked our whole lives for this moment, let's go out there and do it.'"

To Frasor, the fact that Ginyard did not play this year was the one bittersweet memory of winning the national championship. "You want him to be out there on the court with you because he's such a good person, a great player, and just everything you want in a teammate," he said. "It's tough, but at the same time, he was extremely happy when we won."

When that final buzzer rang, Roy Williams couldn't bear to embrace his captain.

"Marcus not playing was the biggest disappointment of the season for me," said Williams. "I started to walk across the floor and hug him," the coach said. "It hit me. I turned away and went on to somebody else and then came back and hugged him later because emotionally, I couldn't handle it. It was and is something I'm very sad about. But my gosh, he's handled it so, so well."

the win," the head coach said. "That's what everybody else should be focused on, too."

Ford, who was to his generation what Hansbrough is to the current generation, arranged to be in Chapel Hill for the game against Evansville. So when Hansbrough tossed in a bank shot with 7:41 left in the first half to break Ford's record, the legend greeted him on the Smith Center court.

The game, a 91–73 victory, was mostly a footnote. The postgame press conference, which included Hansbrough, Ford, and Williams at the same table for a 15-minute chat that touched on virtually every corner of the Carolina Basketball world, belonged in a time capsule.

For three decades, Ford had been the quintessential Tar Heel, not just because of the number of points he scored or the games he won, but because of the determination he showed on the court and the pride he took in being a Carolina Basketball player. That attitude had forever linked him to Dean Smith. The former head coach would never admit to having favorite players, but there was very little question that Ford and Smith had the same special bond that was shared by Ford and the rest of the fan base.

In Hansbrough, Williams had his own Phil Ford, and so did all Carolina Basketball fans of this generation. Like his mentor, Williams would never list favorites. But the connection he had with Hansbrough went beyond coach and ultratalented player.

"I've said many times, no one can ask me about favorite players because it is like picking a favorite child," Williams said. "But what Tyler stood for—not just for Roy Williams, but for college basketball—put him in a different context."

As a longtime Carolina Basketball fan and now as the team's head coach, Williams was uniquely qualified to understand what that context might be.

"Phil Ford set an example for college basketball in what a student athlete should be, what a competitor should be, and what a North Carolina basketball player should be," Williams said. "And for the last four years, [Tyler] has set an example for what a college basketball player should be. It's a guy who can love his university and love his teammates."

"It's always great to come back to North Carolina," Ford said. "This is the greatest college basketball arena in the country. To be a small part of this moment for Tyler is a dream come true for me, and I wouldn't have missed it for the world."

In addition to being one of the greatest Tar Heels ever, Ford remains a devoted fan of the program. After watching the 2008–09 team in person for

the first time, he had high praise for what he thought might be one of the most formidable Carolina teams he had ever seen. The next day, as he boarded a plane to fly to Memphis, where his Charlotte Bobcats had a game against the Grizzlies (Ford had received special dispensation from head coach Larry Brown to miss the team charter), the legendary point guard asked, "Who do we play next?"

Told that the next opponent was Valparaiso, Ford broke into a wide smile.

"I know exactly what they're doing right now," he said.

And what is that?

"Well, if they've already seen film from this year, they're having a whooooole lot of meetings," he said with a wall-shaking laugh.

IN A SOMEWHAT UNUSUAL scheduling quirk, the Tar Heels played two of the next three dog-days games on the road. The first was a trip to Chicago for a date with Valparaiso in the United Center, where the team was greeted with snow on the ground when the charter flight landed.

Phil Ford (left), Tyler Hansbrough (center), and Roy Williams met with the media in a memorable press conference after the Evansville game. (Photo by Jeffrey A. Camarati)

Will Graves averaged four points in the first 20 games. (Photo by Brian Fleming)

Chicagoan Bobby Frasor had lobbied for a team trip to Gibson's, perhaps the most famous steakhouse in the city. Instead, the group decided to hit Dave and Buster's, where the Tar Heels quickly showed the kind of ingenuity and chemistry that would eventually make them national champions. At the sports bar/arcade-type restaurant, one player spotted a guitar accessory used for the Guitar Hero video game, a locker room favorite. "Winning" the guitar required the purchaser to amass 17,000 tickets at the various ticket-producing games—skee ball, a wheel-of-fortune-type game, and many more—in the arcade.

A quick team huddle was called, and all 17 players agreed that together they would try to collect 17,000 tickets. Eric Hoots was in charge of holding the winnings. Less than two hours later, the highly skilled Tar Heels had reached their goal and earned the guitar.

That ended up being the most competitive part of the Chicago trip. As the last game before Christmas, the game against Valpo was the most mentally taxing of the year. Not because of the challenge presented by the Crusaders, but because every player was already looking ahead to the trip home that followed the game. Most were headed straight from the United Center to O'Hare Airport. Williams prefers to give his players several days at home over Christmas, and in the locker room after the 85–63 win, most of them were already checking flight schedules.

Joe Holladay walked around the locker room as the players changed out of their jerseys. "You were already mentally in Los Angeles," he said to Larry Drew II. "You were already in Richmond," he said to Davis. Frasor stood in another corner of the room tying his tie; he had a family wedding to attend across town. Less than 30 minutes after the game ended, very few—if any—of the players could have correctly guessed the final score.

The team would reassemble in Chapel Hill less than a week later to prepare for a home game against Rutgers. That was another dog-days game, as Carolina slogged to a 97–75 victory. The very next day, they were in the air again for a six-hour cross-country flight to Reno, Nevada, a game created by a long-standing relationship between Williams and Wolf Pack head coach Mark Fox.

Bobby Frasor played against Valparaiso in front of his home fans in Chicago. (Photo by Jim Hawkins)

It was a homecoming for basketball staffer Jerod Haase, who has family in Lake Tahoe, but most of the Tar Heels never saw the scenic lake area. Instead, they shuttled between the hotel and the Lawlor Center, where a sellout crowd of 10,526 showed up several hours early on December 31 to see the nation's top-ranked team paste Nevada-Reno, 84–61.

Several family members of Carolina's West Coast players were in attendance, and they were able to hold a brief New Year's Eve celebration before the bus headed straight to the Reno airport.

Noting that the team would be on board an airplane as the ball dropped in Times Square (and on Franklin Street), Deon Thompson smiled. "This is the life of big-time college sports, right?" he said.

The overnight flight put the Tar Heels back at the Smith Center by 6:00 A.M. on New Year's Day. In three days, the true big-time life of Thompson and the Tar Heels would begin: Atlantic Coast Conference play started later that week.

CHAPTER FIVE

Moments of Doubt

"Your attitude will determine your altitude. How tough are we?"

Thought for the Day, January 5, 2009

In a hallway lined with the jerseys of Wake Forest players now playing in the NBA, sophomore Demon Deacon Chas McFarland accepted hugs and high-fives on his way to the team's locker room. McFarland bobbed his head and shouted, "Yeah, baby! We're there!" He meant the fourth-ranked Deacs had officially arrived on the national scene; McFarland's 20 points and nine rebounds were a key part of his team's 92–89 defeat of Carolina.

Just on the other side of a cinder-block wall, the mood was much less boisterous. Roy Williams stood in front of his team and thought that, for the first time in the 2008–09 season, he saw something unexpected.

"I do believe that our team had some doubts for the first time," Williams said. "I think our confidence was shaken a little bit."

It was understandable that it would be shaken. Coupled with a stunning 85–78 home loss to Boston College eight days earlier, the Tar Heels had now lost their first two ACC games for the first time since the 1996–97 season. The consensus preseason favorite now shared last place in the league with Georgia Tech. Even more frustrating, two teams within 90 miles of campus, Duke and Wake Forest, appeared to be among the top national contenders.

And here sat Carolina at 0–2.

"Everybody was thinking maybe we weren't going to be okay," Marcus Ginyard said of the mood in the locker room. "It was like, 'Wow, 0–2, when's the last time that happened? We just got punched in the face by the ACC. What's going on?'"

Williams has Hall of Fame stature because of the sheer quantity of his wins. But much of his success is rooted in his uncanny ability to instantly read the mood in the locker room and gauge the best way to respond to it.

After the Wake Forest loss, however, Williams was not working completely on instinct. Even before entering the room and looking at his players, the head coach had already placed the game in a proper basketball context. He knew the Deacons had shot 47.5% from the field—including 53.6% in the sec-

opposite: Boston College ended Carolina's unbeaten season. (Photo by Jeffrey A. Camarati)

ond half—in front of a school-record home crowd. He knew Mc-Farland played a career game, as did Jeff Teague (34 points). He knew his team shot uncharacteristically poorly, managing just 35.1% from the field and 26.1% from the three-point line. Tyler Hansbrough and Deon Thompson combined to shoot just 6-for-25, and the starting backcourt of Wayne Ellington and Ty Lawson hit just 8-for-25. Lawson notched just one more assist (five) than turnovers (four), and no one on the bench made more than two field goals.

It sounds like the description of a Wake Forest blowout. And yet, with three seconds left, the Tar Heels had the ball and the chance to tie the game. They were out of time-outs because of a mental miscue that forced them to burn one earlier in the game—now *this* was the kind of error that could steam the head coach—but they still got a decent look at the basket, with Will Graves firing a half-court shot that nearly drew iron. There are some losses that require the head coach to kick a trash can. Williams knew this was not one of those games. No matter what the level of concern outside the locker room, to his players he wanted to project the air of a coach whose team had just played poorly on the road and yet somehow lost by only three points to one of the nation's best teams.

"I thought it was extremely important to make sure my confidence [in them] wasn't shaken," Williams said. "It was important for the kids to feel, 'Coach hasn't changed. He still believes in us and he still thinks we're going to be the best.' So that was my attitude.

"The thing is that in basketball, you're always one step from falling off the cliff. I really believe that, and I don't care how good your team is. I wanted to make sure that there was nothing we couldn't come back from in that stretch. It was not a step we would always worry about. It was behind us."

This is what Williams told his team that night. "Guys, we're 0–2 in the league," he said. "Coach Robinson, do you remember our 1991 team at Kansas?"

"I do," Robinson said.

"How did that team start in the conference, Coach Robinson?"

"We were 0–2, Coach."

Carolina shot 28% in the second half at Wake Forest. (Photo by Jim Hawkins)

"And how did that team finish?"

"We played for the national championship," Robinson said.

"We played for the national championship," Williams repeated, looking his players in the eye. "You are good enough to do that. This team is that good. You are that good. If you listen to us and do what we ask you to do, we can be there at the end."

His team believed him. Later, in the afterglow of the national championship, the coach identified that moment as one of the most important on the team's road to Detroit.

"I don't say this very often," Williams said. "But I think that was the wisest thing I did this year. I don't usually talk about 'I,' but that was a big moment to get our kids to understand that if they will just do what we ask them to do, we'll be there at the end. I believed that. I think the kids believed it. That was a huge point in our season from my viewpoint."

"To hear what Coach said and to hear the confidence in his voice when he told us that, and then to look around and see it ringing true even though everyone was obviously very disappointed in our loss, was huge," Ginyard said. "Coach was right, and Coach had confidence in us. We knew we were going to

left: Jeff Teague lit up the Tar Heels for 34 points. (Photo by Jim Hawkins)

center: Danny Green kept Carolina close at Wake Forest with 22 points. (Photo by Jim Hawkins)

right: Deon Thompson slammed home two of his eight points in Winston-Salem. (Photo by Jim Hawkins)

start getting the confidence in ourselves to do what we were capable of doing. We knew we had the potential."

"Everyone was kind of jumping off the ship around us," Bobby Frasor said. "We didn't have any more bandwagon fans. Everyone said, 'Oh, they can't play defense,' but we still believed. And Coach still had faith in us."

The last-place Tar Heels boarded the bus for Chapel Hill mostly in silence. In a few days, they would drop out of the top five in one national poll. Williams, who pays no attention to national polls, didn't mind. On the 90-minute drive home, his thoughts were very different from those of many other Carolina fans across the state.

"What I took back on the bus with me is that we didn't play very well against a team that was really playing well and we almost won," he said. "I knew our team could play better. I was ticked off, as I always am, about losing. But I also felt pretty doggone good because we had a great chance to win that game even though I thought our play stunk."

DESPITE WILLIAMS'S POSTGAME SPEECH, the Tar Heels couldn't simply head home and pack the suitcases for Detroit. The head coach had told his players he believed they could be good enough to play on the last night of the season. That evening was still three months away, and there was substantial improvement to be made before then.

A common thread in the two defeats had been the outstanding offensive performances of the opposing backcourt—and, in guilt by association, the struggling defensive performances of the Tar Heel backcourt. Against Boston College, Tyrese Rice had scored 25 points, Rakim Sanders added 22, and the previously unknown Reggie Jackson hit for 17 off the bench. Against Wake Forest, Teague had exploded for a career-high 34 points. The Tar Heel guards struggled to contain dribble penetration, and once they were beaten by the dribbler, there was very little help defense or rotation coming to assist them.

"I knew Ty could play better, and I knew our team could play better," Williams said. "I knew I was going to have to defend Ty against what people were going to say about what Rice and Teague had done."

"I played horribly in those two games," Lawson said. "I had a bad assist-to-turnover ratio [nine assists and eight turnovers in the two losses]. I took that hard."

Lawson worked on finding remedies for those struggles in two places: in practice with his teammates and in a darkened Smith Center on his own.

In practice, the run-and-shoot sessions—loose individual drills designed to simply keep players sharp during exams and get through the dog days—were mothballed. In their place came some of the most intense practices of the season.

"You could see a change in practice," Lawson said. "Practice was way more intense, a lot longer, and with more defensive competitions."

Losing teams in the defensive competitions faced a tough penalty: lots and lots of running. Losers had to run a 44 or a 55, which is Carolina Basketball–speak for the suicides that used to weed the hopefuls from the contenders in middle-school basketball tryouts. A 55 is simple. A manager puts 55 seconds on the game clock, because even tenths of a second can be important. The players who are required to run assemble on one baseline. When the whistle blows, they have to run the length of the court and back five times in 55 seconds.

On paper, this sounds relatively easy. And maybe, for the first time down the court and back, it is. But even for well-conditioned athletes, that fourth and fifth time down and back can be challenging.

"It was a great motivator," Lawson said. "Those practices were the worst. You really didn't want to lose, because you knew you would end up with two or three 55s in a row, and that's a killer."

Williams had faith that his team could be better defensively. But he also realized there would be a process to reach that improvement. He would have to coach them to it. So he stood on the sideline, blowing his whistle, watching his players run.

After practice was over, most of the players retreated to their dorm rooms and apartments to rest their weary legs. Not Lawson. For the first time in his Carolina career, he became a late-night regular at the Smith Center. When the team arrived back in Chapel Hill from Winston-Salem, he stayed in the gym by himself between 1:00 and 3:00 A.M. to take 500 jumpers on his own. The next two nights, he was joined by some combination of Deon Thompson, Ed Davis, and Justin Watts between 9:00 P.M. and midnight, hoisting 500 jumpers each night.

Lawson's late-night sessions became semiregular occurrences over the remainder of the season, and sometimes he was even joined at the Smith Center by his father. Through that point in the season, he was shooting 52.0% from the field and 43.2% from the three-point line. Over the remainder of the year, he would shoot 54.1% from the field and—more tellingly—50.0% from the three-point line.

"I just needed to get more confidence," Lawson said. "I needed to feel better about my shot. . . . That was the turning point. I started playing harder and started thinking about what I could do to take over the game."

While Lawson was honing his shot, Williams was working on his other backcourt starter's confidence. Wayne Ellington was making less than a third of his three-pointers and was coming off a 4-for-13, three-turnover performance at Wake. The junior sharpshooter had a one-on-one meeting with the head coach.

"Coach told me he wanted me to relax and not think about any pressures that were on me," Ellington said. "He didn't want me to think about anything other than playing basketball. I was thinking the game instead of playing and reacting. That's something that really helped me. I relaxed out there and I started having fun. I enjoyed the game of basketball again."

His enjoyment would help propel Carolina on a series of big victories in what Williams would call the most important stretch of the season.

Practice intensified after two ACC losses. (Photo by Bob Leverone, *The Sporting News*)

CHAPTER SIX

Teetering

"Mental toughness is essential to success."
Thought for the Day,
January 20, 2009

In a year with momentous wins—the Maui title, the blowout at Michigan State, a pair of wins over Duke, and many more—no one expected that the turning point of the season might come during a nondescript stretch of games with an average margin of victory of 21 points.

After losing at Wake Forest, the Tar Heels had to hit the road again later in the week, this time to Virginia. The Cavaliers were struggling, standing just one game over .500 in the league, but they already had an ACC win, which was something the Tar Heels were still seeking. And no matter what quality of team Virginia had, Charlottesville recently had been a tough place for Carolina to win: the Tar Heels hadn't won two straight games there since 1998 and 1999.

"That began the most important stretch of the season," Roy Williams said. "We were teetering a little bit. Our staff was trying to be so positive and take it one game at a time."

The trip got off to an inauspicious start. The Tar Heels usually fly to Charlottesville, using a smaller jet to get into the local airport. Itineraries are e-mailed to every member of the traveling party the day before every road trip. At the top of those itineraries are the words, "Bring your photo ID!" But when the team arrived at Raleigh-Durham International Airport the day before the game in Charlottesville, Wayne Ellington didn't have his ID.

The federal government didn't care that Carolina players are on television nearly 40 times per year and known around the country on sight. No, the Federal Aviation Administration still wanted to see photo identification of everyone on the charter flight—including Ellington.

Occasionally, media guides and game programs can be used as ID substitutes. After all, they always have a photo of the travelers in question plus their name. This time, however, no substitute other than an official ID was acceptable. As his teammates boarded the plane, Ellington was left in the boarding

Ty Lawson had nine assists and no turnovers in UNC's first ACC win. (Photo by Jim Hawkins)

area with Jerod Haase. Rather than take the 45-minute flight, Ellington and Haase would have to make the nearly four-hour drive.

"It was great," Haase said. "It was a time for me to visit with Wayne. We weren't talking X's and O's, but we really had some quality time to visit, and I got to know more about him as a person."

So does that mean Haase will be hiding the ID of one player per trip in the future?

"Well, I think both of us would probably rather have been on the plane," he said. "But it was a drive that we survived without any incident."

Ellington's forgetfulness was one of the few blemishes on an otherwise flawless career. He wasn't always the first to arrive in the weight room, but he wasn't the last, either. He never received a technical foul in his Tar Heel career; his on-court demonstrations were usually limited to a boisterous high-five or perhaps a rare scream of excitement. Almost from birth, his father had been grooming him to be a player eager to take the game's biggest shots. Less known was the role his mother played in refining his social skills and easygoing personality, constantly reminding him to be aware of his surroundings and open to new experiences.

Some observers sometimes mistook that even-tempered demeanor for passivity. In reality, Ellington wasn't even capable of taking time off. After missing a key jumper against Georgetown in the 2007 regional final, he pledged to spend a week away from the gym. The break lasted a little less than that: after about a day, he was back in the Smith Center.

The player who accompanied Haase to Charlottesville was rounding into a more complete player. Virginia did not have the talent to neutralize all of the Carolina options. The Cavaliers chose to double-team Tyler Hansbrough and limited him to just six field goals, but their physical style of play sent him to the free throw line 17 times, where he was successful 15 times.

Lawson added 19 points and nine assists, and his late-night shooting sessions began to pay dividends when he hit all three of his three-point attempts.

"I'm not sure I've seen a better dictated, orchestrated game from a point guard than I did tonight from Ty Lawson," said Virginia coach Dave Leitao. "He was better than advertised."

The Tar Heels built a 50–36 halftime lead and then muddled through the second half on their way to an 83–61 win. The Cavaliers made just 11 of 46 shots from the field in the final 20 minutes.

It might have been just a simple 22-point victory over a struggling, outclassed program. Williams and his coaching staff, who were trying to return the focus to one game at a time, thought it was more than that.

"That's one road win," he told his team in the locker room. "We've gotten back that home game we lost."

The even better news for Ellington, who quietly contributed 13 points, eight rebounds, and five assists (against zero turnovers), was that his driver's license had been delivered to Charlottesville, meaning he could board the return flight home. But Haase's car was still in town, which meant he'd be driving home. Volunteers were recruited for the privilege of riding shotgun and keeping Haase awake on what was certain to be a tiring drive (the game had tipped off at 9:00 P.M., and the Tar Heels didn't clear out of the locker room until close to midnight).

Eric Hoots did not have classes the next day, and he either volunteered or was chosen to accompany Haase, depending on the story you believe. Putting Hoots and Haase in the car together ensured some hijinks. The high temperature that day in Charlottesville had been 30 degrees and the low 14 degrees.

"It was about two or three in the morning," Haase said. "I grew up with two brothers in Lake Tahoe, and it would get awfully cold. We'd always play Freeze-Out in our room, which meant we'd open all the windows, even when it was below freezing, and the last person to put on a blanket was the winner.

"To stay awake on the trip home, Eric and I played Freeze-Out. We rolled down the windows, and the first one to roll up his window was the loser. We split the series. We had to keep playing because at that point, I was pretty tired."

After the Virginia game, Haase changed the heading of each traveling itinerary. Where they had once read, "Bring your photo ID!," they now read, "Bring your photo ID . . . if you want to fly!"

THE FIRST TWO-GAME conference home stand of the season brought something entirely unexpected: standout defensive play.

With ESPN's *Gameday* show in attendance for the second time in

Wayne Ellington scored in double figures 34 times in 2008–09.
(Photo by J. D. Lyon Jr.)

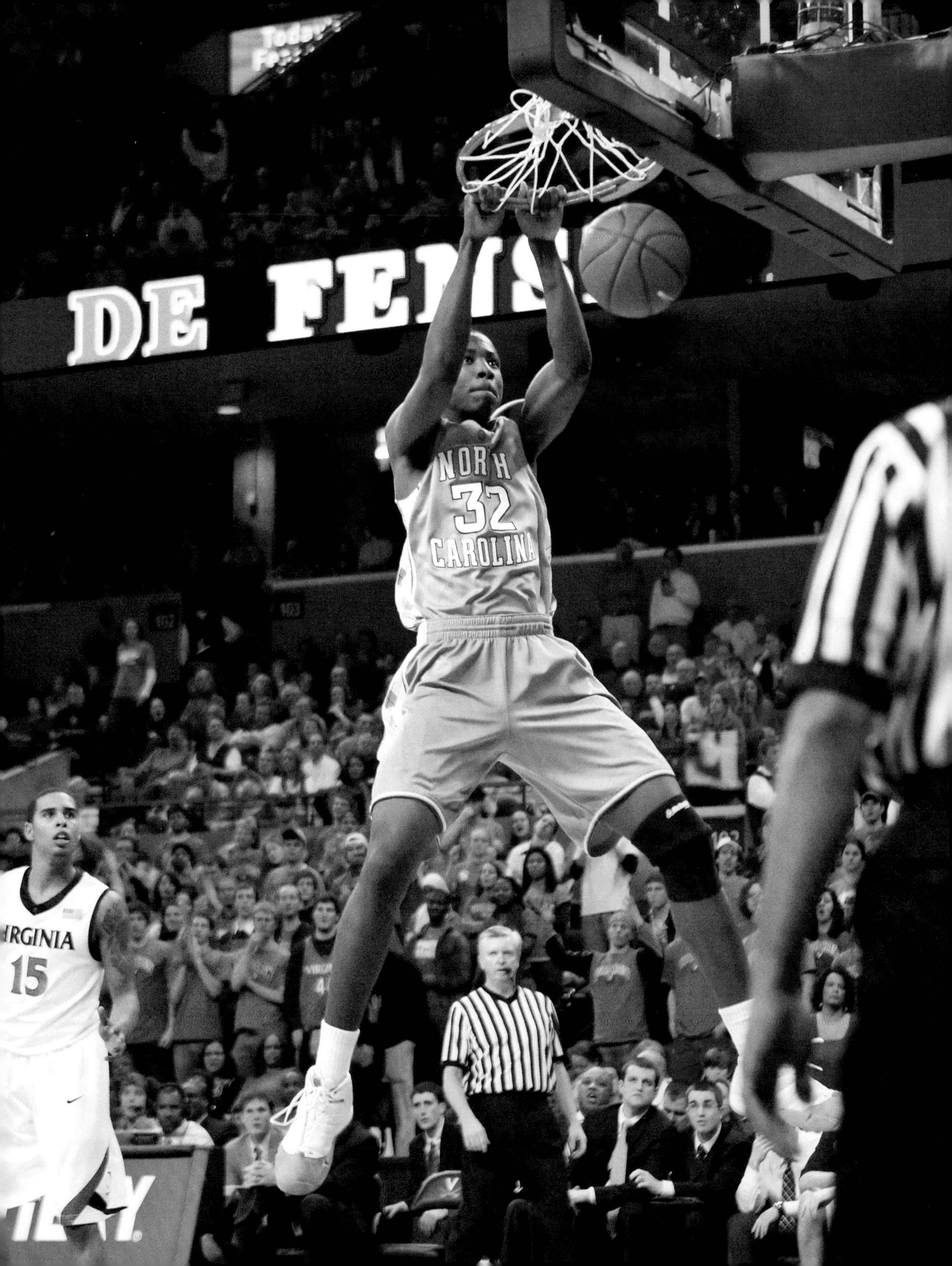
DE FENS
NORTH
32
CAROLINA
VIRGINIA
15

the young season, the Tar Heels hosted a dangerous Miami team that was off to a 13–3 start. The Hurricanes were exactly the type of squad that was supposed to give Carolina trouble, featuring quick, athletic, hot-shooting guards mixed with just enough inside presence. Frank Haith's team already had wins over Ohio State and Maryland, plus road wins at Kentucky and the same pesky Boston College that had whipped the Tar Heels in Chapel Hill.

The best of the Hurricane shooters, Jack McClinton, scored 12 points in the first 12 minutes to help build a 32–23 Miami lead.

"There were times this year when I'd ask our guys, 'Are you bored?'" assistant coach Joe Holladay said. "There were 22,000 people there and we were playing a good ACC team, but it seemed like we were bored."

That's when Lawson showed some of the leadership NBA scouts had demanded of him during his "testing the waters" draft experience the previous summer. Lawson's defense had already helped to stem some of the Hurricanes' momentum. Within a span of 30 seconds midway through the first half, Danny Green had picked up a pair of clean blocks on Miami breakaways. First, he rejected a Dwayne Collins dunk attempt, then he blocked Lance Hurdle's seemingly wide-open layup.

On the second of those blocks, it was Lawson's hustle that created the opportunity for the block. After a Tar Heel turnover, Lawson had sprinted back and bothered Hurdle, forcing him to double-pump. That brief hesitation gave Green an opening, and his block gave some life to a sellout Smith Center crowd.

"They came out playing really well," Green said. "I was trying to make hustle plays to stop them from scoring. Those hustle plays lifted our defense and definitely put the crowd into it. When our crowd's behind us, it makes it a lot easier for us to calm down and play our game and be more confident. A crowd can do that. The momentum of a game can change by your crowd standing up and cheering."

Five minutes later, Lawson's defense became more obvious.

"We weren't playing defense well," he said. "Someone had

Carolina overcame Miami's hot start. (Photo by Robert Crawford)

opposite: Richmond native Ed Davis had six points at Virginia. (Photo by J. D. Lyon Jr.)

to jump-start the defense, and Coach says sometimes that needs to be me. I decided to pressure and see how things went, and it worked out well."

Lawson had good foot speed, solid basketball savvy, and impressive upper-body strength—attributes that could make him a good defensive player, the kind of defender who could control a game from the point-guard position without ever touching the basketball. But he'd rarely been asked to play defense before arriving in Chapel Hill, and he sometimes considered that part of the game a chore.

But the potential was there, and with Marcus Ginyard still relegated to the bench by his foot injury, Lawson's defensive skills were more important than ever. When he decided to attach himself to McClinton, one of the ACC's best players, the impact was immediate. Hurricane post player Jimmy Graham was holding the ball 35 feet from the basket, eager to get rid of it and put McClinton in charge of the offense. But Lawson was shadowing McClinton, denying the pass. Finally, McClinton got close enough to Graham for the big man to attempt a handoff. But Lawson bothered that play, too, and the ball trickled across half-court.

His defense having provided a fresh shot of energy, Lawson then threw himself on the floor to recover the loose ball, went flat on his back, and dropped a two-handed pass to Hansbrough for a momentum-changing dunk.

Miami went scoreless over the final 6:48 of the first half, allowing Carolina to take a 36–32 lead at the break. McClinton, now draped with Lawson, hit just two of his next 10 field-goal attempts.

Everyone in attendance had seen Lawson take over a game with his offense in the past. But watching him seize control with his defense was invigorating.

"Ty set the tone with his pressure," Green said. "He and McClinton were both tired, but Ty didn't give in. He kept pushing and kept pressing."

"The last four or five minutes of the first half were crucial," Williams said. "A key to the game was Ty Lawson's defense late in the first half and in the second half."

Ellington would eventually turn the game into a second-half blowout with a monsoon of three-pointers, his official announcement that he had returned as an offensive threat. But it was his backcourt partner's defensive efforts that kept Carolina in the game long enough to win it.

It was a different kind of win for the Tar Heels, the first time all season they had scored as few as 82 points in a victory. It was also an omen. Just four days later, an unsung effort from another unexpected source would push Carolina over .500 in the league for the first time all season.

DEON THOMPSON'S SIGNATURE PLAYS usually came on offense. Sometimes it was a quick turnaround jumper, other times a slick up-and-under move with a finish off the backboard.

opposite: Deon
Thompson was a
stalwart against
Clemson. (Photo
by Bob Donnan)

He didn't block many shots—the primary stat-sheet measure of a defensive big man for most fans—so his defense rarely drew attention. Partially as a result of having to defend Carolina's bevy of talented posts every day in practice, Thompson had turned into a capable defender. He understood how to use his bulk to push opponents away from the basket and knew how to defend early in the possession to avoid being pinned on the low block.

He would need all of those skills against Clemson's Trevor Booker, who Tar Heel players considered one of the toughest matchups in the league because of his combination of quickness and muscle.

"Booker is one of the strongest players in the conference," Hansbrough said. "He's really explosive. When you can jump like he jumps, it makes up for any lack of height."

The primary story line any time Clemson comes to UNC is Carolina's dominance of the series in Chapel Hill; another victory would push the Tar Heel advantage to 54–0, the longest such streak in the nation. But Tiger head coach Oliver Purnell was quietly building a solid program in football country and had made his team into a squad that was a threat no matter where the game was played. Clemson preferred a trapping, fast-paced style of play and had the offensive weapons to outscore many foes.

"I thought the Clemson game would tell us a lot more about our team," assistant coach Steve Robinson said. "It was a pivotal time period for us. We had beaten Clemson so many times. Clemson had played us tough three times last year, and now we had to go out and do it again."

The Tiger attack depended on an inside-outside combination, with Booker drawing defensive attention to allow the Clemson shooters to have open three-point looks. Try to cover Booker with just one man, and he was likely to score; he would eventually become the first player to lead the ACC in both field-goal percentage and rebounding since Tim Duncan. He'd posted double-doubles in all three meetings with the Tar Heels during the 2007–08 season, pulling down a staggering 18 offensive rebounds in those three games.

It was Thompson's assignment to neutralize the Clemson big man. The results: just 3-of-6 for Booker from the field (his second-fewest shot attempts in any ACC game), four rebounds (just one offensive), and seven points.

Thompson did most of his work before Booker ever caught the ball, which meant it largely went unnoticed. But every time the big Tiger would try to

Tyler Hansbrough bent a tooth but played on against Clemson. (Photo by Peyton Williams)

clear room on the low block, Thompson was already there, pushing him out a step, trying to make him catch the ball in an area that was uncomfortable.

"I had to do my defensive work early," Thompson said. "Once he catches the ball, he's a beast, so I wanted to make it tough for him to catch the ball. I tried to front him and wall him off in the post. When he got the ball, my teammates did a great job with helping down."

As usual, the battle was extremely physical. A first-half collision left one of Hansbrough's teeth bent backwards in his mouth. It wasn't loose, it was bent. He was taken to the locker room to allow a physician to evaluate it. "I think you need to let a dentist take a look at this," he told Hansbrough.

Down the hall, the echoes of the still-close game—the halftime lead was just five points—could be heard. Hansbrough had no time for a dentist.

"No!" he screamed. "Look at it after the game!" He grabbed his tooth, bent it back to its normal position, picked up a mouth guard, stormed back onto the court and announced he was ready to reenter the fray.

Once again, it was the Carolina defense that kept the game close long enough for the offense to take control. Eventually, as he always seemed to do against Clemson, Ellington surged, and the Tar Heels cruised to a 94–70 victory. It was Ellington's second straight game with at least 20 points, the first time in his career he'd had such gaudy back-to-back scoring outputs, but he knew where the real credit belonged.

"With Deon, you have to watch closely to see all those little things he's doing," Ellington said. "It's fun to see him do things like that in areas where he has improved so much."

Green Perseveres, Excels

Danny Green might like to dance, but he was tired of being best known for his pregame routine and not his play on the court.

As a lark during his time as a reserve, Green created his signature dance. Soon, he was doing it before every home game as the Smith Center's sound system blasted House of Pain's "Jump Around" just prior to tip-off. Gyrating in front of more than 20,000 fans in Chapel Hill certainly made people take notice, but Green entered his final college season longing to be recognized instead for his skills with the basketball.

As a junior during the Final Four run of 2008, Green developed into perhaps the nation's best sixth man, good for instant offense off the bench. He finished fourth on the team in scoring and was just the second Carolina reserve since 1994 to average in double figures. Even though he started just one game in his first three seasons, Green became productive enough on the court to enter his name in the 2008 NBA Draft before returning to school.

Still, reporters seemed to focus more on Green's pregame dance ritual than on his on-court prowess.

"It was a lot of fun on the sidelines, having fun with those guys, but it wasn't something that I wanted to be remembered by," Green said. "That's something that I've always worked on growing up—you know, not just being a shooter or a ball-handler or a defensive guy, but being a basketball *player*."

Even if the media were slow to recognize it, Green had become well-rounded on the floor—a "stat-sheet stuffer," as his coaches dubbed him. During the off-season, Roy Williams and his staff had strongly considered inserting Green in the starting lineup, even if Marcus Ginyard hadn't suffered a stress fracture in his foot.

"I've always liked his game and liked what he brought to the table and thought he could produce if he had the minutes and the confidence," said C.B. McGrath. "Obviously, this year speaks for itself. He was third team All-ACC and just had a great year."

Green finished his career having played in more games (145) and wins (123) than any other Tar Heel in history, tying for second in ACC history in victories. He was the only player in ACC history to compile at least 1,000 points, 500 rebounds, 250 assists, 150 three-pointers, 150 blocked shots, and 150 steals, reflecting his varied skills. He is among the top 10 at UNC in three-pointers made and free-throw percentage.

Danny Green scored 1,368 points as a Tar Heel. (Photo by Jim Hawkins)

"From the beginning, he had a lot of adjusting to do with Coach Williams and in the system we have here," Jerod Haase said. "Over time, he did adjust. By senior year, I think he started to shine and got that opportunity to play more minutes and start and really came through."

By the end of the season, Green had earned a spot on the ACC's All-Defensive Team after struggling as a defender early in his career. He finished eighth in school history in blocked shots with 155 and is the only small forward among the top 10 on the list.

"The biggest key for Danny was making better decisions," said Williams. "His assist-error ratio was really good all year long. He stopped taking as many chances. He stopped making as many silly plays, driving the baseline."

After entering his final campaign with only six more assists than turnovers in three years, Green was far more efficient as a senior, compiling a career-high 104 assists against 63 turnovers.

The transition from sixth man to starter wasn't as easy as it seemed, however.

"I wasn't used to starting," Green admitted. "As a high schooler, of course, you're the star on your team, you're playing a lot. But starting here was different. So it was an adjustment for me. Coming off the bench, I was able to . . . see how the game was being played, how the referees were calling calls, and who I was going to be guarding. . . . But, being a starter, you have to know all of that from the jump."

Green was a quick study in the starting lineup and was a joy for Carolina fans to watch throughout the season. He scored a career-high 26 points in Maui against Chaminade in the fourth game of the year. The next day, he poured in 21 against Oregon, hitting five three-pointers. Five nights later, against UNC Asheville in Chapel Hill, he drilled six in a row from behind the arc, the last of which he launched from just across midcourt.

"I didn't know how deep I was," Green said of the long-range shot, laughing. "I was pretty far out, I just caught the ball and it was a heat check. When I caught it, if I'm open, I'm going to shoot it." The quick success eased his transition to being a starter.

"He's got some of the best hands that I've ever coached," said Joe Holladay. "If you look at deflections and blocked shots and timing and all those things, he was one of those guys that would make the big basket. The one that drove the dagger in there usually came from Danny."

Green's big plays—whether they were jump shots, steals, or blocked

Green played in four wins at Duke. (Photo by Kevin Cox, Getty Images)

shots—seemed to come just when the Tar Heels needed a spark. Against LSU in the NCAA second round, his three-pointer with 6:30 to play gave Carolina a 70–63 lead, UNC's biggest since just after halftime.

"Danny has a tendency to take the gutsiest shots of anybody I've ever played with," said Tyler Hansbrough. "Wayne saved it, he kicked it right back to DG, and Danny hit that three. I thought that was where we kind of put the hammer down, and . . . had the game in control."

The season wasn't without setbacks for Green, who went 3 for 25 in a pair of frustrating ACC Tournament games. He never lost faith in himself, however, bouncing back with 15 points and 10 rebounds in the NCAA first-round win over Radford and scoring in double figures in four of six NCAA contests.

The starting role on a national-championship team was made all the sweeter for Green because his father, who had been incarcerated and unable to attend Danny's games for two seasons, was in the crowd for most of his son's outings as a senior. While his dad was away, the younger Green took over much of the responsibility for raising his two younger brothers back home in New York.

"For him to be around to support me throughout the season definitely meant a lot," Green said of his father's presence. "It made it easier for me to just relax and play my game and not worry about all the off-the-court distractions. It was definitely a distraction—how my family was doing, how I was going to take care of them. . . . But now that he's home and he's been able to watch my games, I know everything's fine."

Green's perseverance didn't go unnoticed.

"There's nobody that you have to look at and respect more than Danny Green," said Marcus Ginyard. "It's something that everybody's always going to remember, the fact that Danny continued to play at such an elite level despite all the things that he's been through."

CHAPTER SEVEN

Road Warriors

"The difference between ordinary and extraordinary is that little extra."

Thought for the Day, January 30, 2009

The senior class of Danny Green, Bobby Frasor, Tyler Hansbrough, Mike Copeland, and Marcus Ginyard set most of the four-year Carolina Basketball records. They won more games than any other group in the program's storied history. But their most remarkable achievement occurred in a 32-game subset of that four-year career. Over the last four seasons, the Tar Heels compiled a 25–7 Atlantic Coast Conference road record—a mark equal to or better than the *home* record of every other program in the league.

In an era when even one or two road victories are considered strong NCAA Tournament credentials, Hansbrough's class became the rarest of college basketball specimens: an overwhelming road favorite.

"I believe the kids have adopted the attitude of, 'Boy, this is fun going into their living room and beating them,'" Williams said. "I think they agree with me that just because we're playing somewhere else doesn't mean we shouldn't play well. Just because we're playing somewhere else doesn't mean the other team is going to win anyway, so we don't have to box out.

"I think some teams are beaten mentally [on the road] before the game starts. I never want my teams beaten before the game starts. Our kids believe we can beat you anytime, anywhere, anyplace, anyhow. When teams play us at home, we're one of a few teams that the other team has to wonder if their home crowd will be enough."

Every ACC venue has its quirks. Maryland is probably the rowdiest. At Duke, the students are the closest. And at Florida State, one of the few schools in the league where basketball takes a backseat to football, beer is served at the off-campus facility and the student section is known to fill up in the second half if the Seminoles are playing a nationally ranked team close.

Late in the game against Carolina, that student section was starting to press toward the court. The Seminoles held a 77–74 lead and had the ball with 1:24 remaining. Just seconds before, FSU head coach Leonard Hamilton used the arena PA system to warn his fans against throwing objects on the court.

Now, with the Tar Heels on the ropes, the PA announcer made the following announcement: "This is a reminder that ACC rules prohibit anyone other than game participants from being on the court after the game. Please stay off the court after the game."

The implication was obvious. Once Florida State pulled the upset, stay off the floor.

But Williams decided to change his defense, sending a trap at the very talented Toney Douglas to force him to relinquish the ball. The Seminoles had other good players, but Douglas was the star. If someone was going to toss in a backbreaking shot, Williams wanted it to be someone other than Douglas.

Ty Lawson and Wayne Ellington double-teamed Douglas on the sideline, while Green watched, one pass away.

When Douglas tried to pass, Green got the steal; he then made a layup, was fouled, and made the free throw. It was a five- or six-point swing in less than five seconds, and it was the kind of veteran play a winning road club always makes. No panic, just fundamentals.

"I was lucky to be in the right spot at the right time," Green said. "They could have just held the ball and waited for us to foul, but we ran a trap at them and I was the interceptor. I got there at the right time, and I thought the guy was going to let me go because that would have been the smarter play and they were up by three."

"That might have been a season-turning play," Hansbrough said.

Equally important was Hansbrough's man-to-man defense on Douglas, as switches left the forward—who already had four fouls—on the deadly Douglas twice in the closing minutes.

"To be honest with you, I was comfortable because I've guarded Ty Lawson in practice," Hansbrough said. "There's no way Toney Douglas is as quick or as fast as Ty, so I'm used to that speed. I gave him a little ground and used my length, and whenever he went up to shoot, I was lucky and got a little piece of the ball."

Hansbrough's "luck"—mixed with a healthy dose of solid defensive fundamentals—stymied Douglas twice. That left Carolina with the ball out of bounds, 94 feet from the hoop, with 3.2 seconds left.

The Tar Heels practice a play for that exact situation, a play that Williams taught his team during the very first week of practice when this year's seniors were freshmen. It's designed not to get a shot, but to get the ball to midcourt in just one pass and allow the Tar Heels to call a time-out. In general, Williams likes his chances of scoring from half-court in two seconds better than his chances of scoring from full-court in three seconds.

Knowing that road success depends on execution, Williams called for that play. But also realizing that winning on the road often requires adaptability, the head coach grabbed his point guard on the way out of the huddle.

"If the play's not there," he told Lawson, "go with it."

Hansbrough made the trigger in-bounds pass. "The play was that I was supposed to throw it to half-court," he said. "But I thought, 'Even if that guy is open, I'm giving it to Ty,' because I knew Ty could go the length of the court."

So Hansbrough ignored Green, who was indeed wide open at half-court. Instead, he found Lawson, whose speed puts him in a very small group of Tar Heel point-guard jets that includes Kenny Smith and Raymond Felton. Law-

Ty Lawson's game-winning three at Florida State. (Photo by Mike Erdelyi)

son blitzed down the court, needing just four dribbles to go from one three-point line to the other. He then elevated off one foot and took a shot. The horn sounded a blink after Lawson released the ball, and he had already landed by the time it swished through the net.

"I saw I had a lane to the basket," Lawson said. "I looked up at the clock, saw there was one second left, and let it go. That was the first time since we've been here that we hit a game-winner with the clock at zero."

In fact, it was the first time Carolina had hit a game winner as time expired since Brendan Haywood did it against Charlotte on December 12, 1998.

Soon, Lawson was wrapped in a giant bear hug from Hansbrough, who had sprinted down the court as he watched the flight of the winning shot. Wil-

liams remained composed as he shook hands with Hamilton and the rest of
the Seminoles, but inside he knew it was an important win.

"That's two road wins," he told his team in the locker room. "We got the
home loss back that we had against Boston College, and now we've got one
more."

SINCE WILLIAMS'S RETURN to Carolina, his reshaping of the Carolina-Duke
rivalry has drawn most of the in-state attention. After struggling against the
Blue Devils in the early part of the decade, the Williams-led Tar Heels have
claimed six of the last seven meetings in the nation's best sports rivalry.

But Williams grew up in an era when Carolina's biggest in-state rival was

NC State, not Duke. His senior season at UNC coincided with the beginning of State's best stretch in the modern era, as the Wolfpack won nine straight games against the Tar Heels from February 29, 1972, through January 18, 1975. That stretch included the 1974 national title for Norm Sloan's State team, and it looked as if the Pack was about to reclaim the dominant position they had held in ACC basketball through the Everett Case era in the early 1950s.

Williams knew all of this history. He also knew that the main difference in the Carolina-Duke games and Carolina-State games was the degree of passion involved. The loser of the Carolina-Duke game usually retained a chance at national honors. But lose to NC State, and it was almost certain to end up on the cover of the Wolfpack's media guide the next season. Reynolds Coliseum was one of the toughest, loudest, foulest places in the league to play (the program moved to the more sterile RBC Center in 1999).

Williams's passion for winning on the road is built on the idea of watching a rowdy crowd go quiet, of knowing that simply pointing at the scoreboard can silence a merciless student section. During his formative years as a Tar Heel, for all of these reasons and others, Williams came to believe that there is simply no more enjoyable place to win on the road than at NC State. The Wolfpack's slide in national prominence coincided with Williams's departure for Kansas, and he missed almost two decades' worth of struggles. That meant that when he returned to Chapel Hill, his view of the rivalry hadn't been lessened by some of the routs of the 1990s.

"He always gives this speech in shootaround before we play State," Tyler Hansbrough said. "He's in a bad mood. He's blunt with you. If you ask him a question, he'll give you a straight-up, short answer. It's like he's pissed off because we have to play State. I'm like, 'We have to play State, Coach. It's two games a year. We have to play them.' And for those two games, before practice or before shoot-

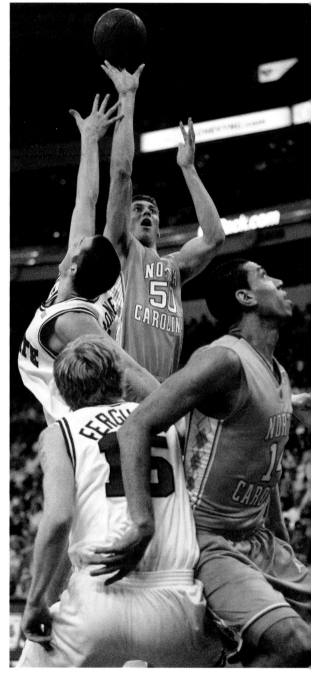

Tyler Hansbrough scored 63 points in his last two games at NC State. (Photo by Jim Hawkins)

opposite: Roy Williams has won 12 of 13 meetings against NC State since he returned to the Tar Heel bench. (Photo by Jim Hawkins)

around, he's just mad because we have to play them. And he doesn't wear red, either."

Hansbrough is right. Since Williams became head coach of Carolina in the fall of 2003, not one single day has he been spotted in a red shirt. That's a love and respect for the rivalry that even a State fan can appreciate.

Fittingly, Williams found a kindred spirit in Hansbrough. At Duke, the students try to be creative with their taunts. At State, creativity is discouraged and sign making encouraged. On January 12, 2008, when the Wolfpack baseball team was being honored during a time-out of another UNC-State battle, one member of the team waved a sign featuring a photo of Hansbrough after Gerald Henderson's elbow had sent bright red blood spewing from his nose. The sign read: "Hansbrough finally wearing the right color."

The sign was wildly applauded, of course. And Carolina won the game, of course.

UNC outscored the Pack, 46–16,
in the paint. (Photo by J. D. Lyon Jr.)

Over Hansbrough's career, the State students have made signs comparing him to a Muppet and signs with pointed comments about his mother. They have also watched him compile an 8–1 record against their team, the only defeat being a 2007 misstep that still galls him.

"I would say NC State's at the top of my list," Hansbrough said. "It's because of their fans. It seems like they never leave you alone. Everywhere you go, they're hassling you, and when they beat us, they stormed the court and yelled at us and got in our face. That's the kind of thing you remember through your whole career, and you want to prove yourself and prevent that from ever happening again. That's something that has driven me every single game we've played State."

And yet: "I think Coach Williams probably hates State more than I do."

"Definitely," Deon Thompson said. "He'd rather beat State than eat."

As Carolina has controlled the series with the Wolfpack, even NC State's building has turned more friendly. Each year, more fans wearing Carolina blue creep into the arena, and at least two of the RBC Center suites are usually packed with Tar Heel fans. This year's game in Raleigh was the most low-key in the recent history of the rivalry, as only a late-game altercation between Ben McCauley and Copeland gave any indication that this was supposed to be a blood feud.

The Tar Heels shot nearly 60 percent from the field and were never in real danger, eventually beating the Pack for the 11th time in the last 12 tries. Hansbrough continued his mastery of the RBC Center, scoring 31 points and ending his RBC career averaging 23.6 points and 7.8 rebounds per game in the hated building.

Hansbrough's brother in disliking NC State, Williams, was suitably pleased with the victory.

"I love that spot," he said with a grin. "I love getting those people to the parking lot early."

4-0

For Carolina's senior class, winning one game at Cameron Indoor Stadium seemed improbable. Winning two seemed unlikely. Three, an aberration.

But winning four, a clean sweep of the home court at rival Duke, seemed impossible. Not because one team was clearly better than the other. Carolina was ranked third in the nation, Duke sixth. The Tar Heels were 21–2, the Blue Devils 20–3. Each team had a pair of losses in the league. On paper, they seemed evenly matched.

But several intangibles resided in Durham. There was no way—none—that Duke was going to let the Hansbrough-led Tar Heels go undefeated at Cameron. Not at the arena where fans camp out for months, where students chant "Our House!" just to remind opponents that wins there are rare. Over the previous seven seasons, Duke had suffered just eight home losses; they sported another unblemished home record when they tangled with the Tar Heels on February 11. Only two players, Wake Forest's Tim Duncan and Rusty LaRue, had played in and won four straight games at Cameron in the nearly 30-year Mike Krzyzewski era.

Since the two-game road winning streak, Roy Williams's team had won two more ACC games—a 17-point whipping of Maryland and a 15-point defeat of Virginia. Those victories were barely a blip on the national radar. In fact, the Tar Heels made more news off the court when it was announced that Marcus Ginyard would miss the remainder of the season and seek a medical redshirt, and Will Graves had been suspended for the remainder of the season.

The Ginyard decision had been building for weeks, and his teammates had watched him in pain during practice. They knew it was a possibility he could miss the entire season. The Graves news was more sudden, and it abruptly removed a player from the rotation who had worked his way into an important role. At Williams's behest, Graves had lost 37 pounds since his arrival in Chapel Hill, and even though he wasn't shooting as well as he had as a freshman, his defense and court savvy—areas that had previously needed work and led to reduced playing time—had improved to the point that even when he wasn't shooting well, he still contributed. His absence was another depletion of the depth that was supposed to be a Tar Heel strength.

It wasn't quite the dog days when attrition had forced Williams to shuffle his rotation, but it was that early part of the conference schedule when every game hasn't quite developed the critical feeling of most February and March contests. In an effort to make sure his team wasn't just coasting from big game to big game, the head coach devised some creative practice plans in mid-January.

"We wanted to make sure the guys enjoyed the ride all year long," he said. "So we split the team up, half on one end and half on the other. And we told them it was a free-throw-shooting contest, that they had to make one-and-ones. And then we said, 'Oh, and you have to shoot these with your eyes closed.' Then we did one competition where they had to bank in their free throws. Then we had a dribbling race where the guys had to put their arm around a partner and they each had to dribble with their free hand. We wanted to let the kids know it still had to be fun."

No extra incentives were needed during the week of the Duke game. With the year's first installment of the rivalry game approaching—which, as always, came complete with blanket ESPN coverage and now had the new addition of a one-hour HBO documentary exclusively devoted to Carolina-Duke— Williams was aware of the mounting tide of momentum building against his team. So at practice the day before the game, he gathered his squad in a circle at midcourt before drills began.

"They're saying we're not going to beat them," he told his team. "They're saying the streak stops right here."

He looked around at Hansbrough and Green and Frasor, the three players to whom he knew the streak was probably the most meaningful.

"The streak doesn't stop just because they say so," he said. "We've got a hand in this, too. They don't know how well we're going to play."

To Williams, one of the most powerful motivators for a talented team is the feeling that they are an underdog. He believes feeling like an underdog is worthless if the team doesn't have the talent, but give him a solid team that believes everyone is against them, and more often than not he'll find a way to motivate them to victory.

"It was a little bit of me trying to build their confidence," he said of that speech at practice. "But I also really believed it. I really thought Duke was

going to say, 'We're going to show them. We're going to get them this time. We're not going to let them come in our building and beat us.'"

THE COACH WAS RIGHT. One of the unique features of the Tobacco Road rivalry is the mutual respect shared by both programs. They are completely different and have grown even more starkly different since Williams's return to Chapel Hill. Mike Krzyzewski doesn't golf; Williams loves it. Krzyzewski is a wine connoisseur who added a wine cellar to his home; Williams doesn't drink. It's true that at Carolina, as the popular T-shirt says, basketball is life. At Duke, Tar Heel fans often perceive that life is basketball, that the willingness to spend 45 days in a tent camping out for admission to a basketball game might be more of a commentary on other entertainment options than on a fan's dedication to his or her team.

But there is still the underlying feeling that even if one side loses a game to the other, it's not because the opponent cheated or didn't deserve it. It's simply because these are two of the best programs in college basketball, and one side has to lose. The way the programs go about reaching their goals may be very different, but their achievements are often very similar.

This year, though, an edgy frustration was slightly evident in Durham for the first time. At 7:00 P.M., two hours before the 9:00 P.M. tip-off, the tent dwellers of Krzyzewskiville were busy getting into costume and getting their faces painted. Duke students don't simply wear the typical college student uniform of khaki shorts and school T-shirts to basketball games. Some dress up as Vikings. Others prefer a superhero-type devil suit. Most have royal blue body paint somewhere on their skin.

Intruders are not welcome, which is what a group of ten UNC undergraduates discovered when they tried to walk through the tent city. They made the mistake of starting a pro-Carolina chant. A few minutes later, they were covered in royal blue, white, and black paint. A crowd of hundreds of students waiting in line to gain entry broke ranks and followed the UNC students, with a handful of poor decision makers ripping open trash bags to get empty bottles to fire at the offending Tar Heels.

That's the kind of aggression that is born of desperation, which is why it's usually seen more frequently at other less-successful schools. That it had now taken up residence in Durham was a sort of backwards tribute to Hansbrough's class.

But Williams's guess about the emotion of the evening was right. Deon Thompson kept the Tar Heels in the game early, scoring 10 points in the first seven minutes, and Frasor hit three first-half three-pointers. But Duke played an almost perfect first half, shooting 61.8% from the field and 66.7% from the three-point line. That qualified as a major offensive explosion for a Duke team that had averaged just 66 points per game in its previous four ACC games. Carolina had struggled to defend Duke's curl, and Jon Scheyer had 11 points at halftime.

Williams was happy that, despite the scoring outburst, his team trailed just 52–44. His players, however, were less pleased. The coaching staff traditionally meets as a group at the beginning of halftime, allowing the coaches to compose their halftime message and the players to decompress from the first 20 minutes of action.

"Come on!" Hansbrough yelled as he entered the cramped visitors' locker room. "We can play better than this. This is *not* good enough!" By the time he finished his rant, he was standing up facing his teammates, coming very close to literally pulling out his hair.

Thompson joined the fray, barking, "We can play better, guys. We're going to be okay."

Then something unexpected happened. Mike Copeland had watched with growing frustration as Duke scored seemingly at will. As a North Carolina native, he'd been indoctrinated into Carolina Basketball at an early age by watching Tar Heel games on television with his grandmother. As a prepster in Winston-Salem, he patiently waited for a UNC scholarship offer while explaining to other interested schools that he wanted to try to be a Tar Heel, even if that desire cost him a chance at their school. He still earnestly admitted to occasionally having to pinch himself to verify that he was indeed a UNC basketball player.

His constant good humor and ever-present grin endeared him to everyone on campus, but he had one of the deepest understandings of Tobacco Road rivalries of anyone on the roster. Unlike anyone else in the room, he actually remembered watching Duncan and LaRue. That frustration, combined with his teammates' obvious disappointment, built into an explosion. The senior kicked a chair, sending it bouncing off a locker and nearly ricocheting into Thompson.

"We were supposed to be playing better, and I was upset," Copeland said. "Everybody thought that I threw the chair, but really I kicked it. Fortunately, it didn't hit anybody. But it did seem to light a fire in everybody."

With his players having already taken care of the emotional appeals, that left Williams free to spend his time on the more technical aspects of crafting a comeback.

When the coaches entered the locker room, Williams stepped to the chalkboard and diagrammed the play Duke had used with such success in the first 20 minutes, with a guard coming around a high screen 15 to 17 feet from the basket for a jump shot.

"Guys, we have to do a better job on this," he told his team. "On this play, our big guy has to get higher. The high screener has to help. The perimeter player has to find an easy path to come through. We can't just let him curl right through the middle of the lane. You've got to be there in his face."

Deon Thompson had 10 first-half points at Duke. (Photo by Bob Leverone, *The Sporting News*)

Deon Thompson reminded the Crazies of the streak as he exited the floor. (Photo by Robert Crawford)

opposite: Ty Lawson dominated the second half at Cameron. (Photo by Bob Leverone, *The Sporting News*)

In the second half, the Tar Heels were in his face. Duke's shooting percentage plummeted to 36.1% and they made just 2-of-15 three-pointers.

"That was what we needed to do to win that game," Lawson said. "We needed our bigs to step out and contest shots. When we played defense, it made the game a lot easier. Once we started playing defense, it was contagious."

Duke missing field goals finally created transition opportunities for Lawson, who had never played in a loss to the Blue Devils. Duke briefly held a 56–48 second-half lead, but a Hansbrough jumper and Lawson's full-court heroics keyed a 25–11 spurt.

Then, over the closing minutes of the second half, Lawson scored nine of Carolina's points in a 12–0 run, with many of them coming off dribble penetration and spectacular, twisting baskets. They would go in the scorebook as layups, but normally the diminutive point guard had to fend off contact and spin the ball off the backboard to have a chance at two points.

It looked improvised, but it was actually the culmination of a lifetime of practice.

"When I was younger, I used to like to do reverse layups," Lawson said. "I learned how to put English on the ball so it will roll into the basket. Sometimes Danny [Green] and I will mess around with it in practice, seeing how we can spin the ball in. I feel like how strong I am is underrated because I take a lot of contact when I go to the basket."

Hansbrough contributed the other three points during Lawson's personal run, nailing a three-pointer that was the perfect bookend to a similar three-pointer he had nailed as a freshman.

The Tar Heel lead eventually ballooned to 88–71 with 3:42 remaining, and a late offensive flurry pushed the final margin to 101–87. It was the first time an opponent had scored 100 points against Duke in a regulation game at Cameron since Carolina did it in 1983.

The victory would be followed by a raucous celebration in the locker room, where all the chairs were safely tucked away from Copeland. In what had become an annual tradition, Eric Hoots sprinted from his lofty perch in the Cameron crow's nest, where he had operated the team's video equipment, and exchanged boisterous chest bumps with every member of the team.

For the players, though, the most memorable part of the celebration took place on the court rather than in the locker room.

"They're so loud when the game starts," Hansbrough said. "If you tried to read a book out loud at the start of the game, there's no way you could hear

left: Tyler Hansbrough scored 76 points in four wins at Duke. (Photo by Jim Hawkins)

right: Roy Williams has led UNC to six wins in its last seven games against the Blue Devils. (Photo by Jim Hawkins)

opposite: Carolina shot 54.8% at Duke. (Photo by Bob Leverone, *The Sporting News*)

Roy Williams and Joe Holladay enjoying a post-Duke victory meal. (Photo by Bob Leverone, *The Sporting News*)

yourself. That's how loud they are when we go out for warm-ups. But after the game, when we're leaving the court, you could probably go to midcourt and read a book and everyone in the stands could hear you. That's how quiet it gets."

"They talk trash," Lawson said. "They get right up in your face and they do that thing with their fingers. So on the way off the court, I did the spirit fingers back to them. They were looking at me like I was crazy."

Frasor, who continued his stellar play against Duke, shook his head as he pulled on his dress shirt.

"It still feels surreal," he said. "Any other Carolina player who loses at Duke, I'm going to look at them and say, 'I never did that.'"

CHAPTER NINE

Meltdown

"Reputation is a large bubble that bursts when you try to blow it up yourself."

Thought for the Day, February 16, 2009

The problem with the apocalyptic annual buildup to the first Carolina-Duke game of the season—the first game almost always receives more hype than the second one, largely because the first meeting serves as the unofficial opening of college basketball for the part of the nation that is less obsessed with the sport than Tobacco Road—is that when it's over, there are more regular-season games to play before the postseason. After winning at Cameron Indoor Stadium, it feels as if a team should advance straight to March.

But that wasn't the order of the Tar Heel schedule. Instead, they first had to travel to Miami, where Ty Lawson played through an illness that almost kept him out of the game entirely to score 17 of his 21 points in the second half, Danny Green picked up a key block on Jack McClinton, Tyler Hansbrough took a key charge in the game's final minute to preserve the victory, and a ninth-straight league win gave Carolina a two-game ACC lead in the loss column. At almost any other time on the schedule, it might have felt like a turning point. Instead, coming just four days after the Duke game, it felt more like a chore.

And never had the NC State rivalry felt more like an afterthought than the next week in the Smith Center, when a 14–0 second-half run expanded a three-point halftime advantage and the Tar Heels cruised to an 89–80 victory. The most notable aspect of the win was the return of Tyler Zeller, who had made a speedy recovery from his fractured wrist and worked his way into being part of the post rotation over the final month of the season.

Just a month earlier, it had seemed all the off-court news had been bad for the Tar Heels. Now, good fortune seemed to have returned, which means what happened next might have been expected.

"We got fat and happy," Lawson said.

They didn't start the February 21 game against Maryland fat and happy. They actually started very well, building a 52–36 lead with 14:17 left in the second half. The sellout crowd at the Comcast Center was desultory, and Mary-

land players were chiding each other on the court. It seemed easy. Too easy, perhaps.

"We went brain dead for a while," Williams said. "All year long, we had worked on time and score situations in practice. We hadn't had many of them in games, but whether it was Miami or Florida State, we had done some nice things in late-game situations. Then, all of a sudden at Maryland, it was like we forgot our brain for about four or five minutes."

The struggles began with turnovers against the Maryland press. The Terrapins apply consistent pressure, and to that point it had been largely insignificant. Suddenly, though, the Tar Heels got loose with the ball. After a couple of ill-advised shots and turnovers by Carolina, the Terps had put together a 10–2 run that got them back in the game and reignited the slumbering crowd.

In a time-out later in the game, Williams looked at his team.

"Okay, guys," he said. "We're playing two opponents. We're playing Maryland and we're playing the clock."

Even late, even after Maryland had tried to come back, Carolina held a 73–65 lead with less than four minutes to play. But, just like in the loss at Wake Forest, some uncharacteristically questionable offense—missed free throws, bad decisions, and rushed plays—cracked open the door for the Terps.

"On our last four or five possessions, if we would've just taken a shot-clock violation, we would've won the game," Williams said.

That's not what happened. Greivis Vasquez, who had been kryptonite to Lawson in the past, posted a triple-double and made a game-tying basket with eight seconds to play in regulation. Vasquez also tossed in a three-pointer with 1:15 left in overtime and nailed a pair of free throws with 5.4 seconds left to provide the final 88–85 margin.

"We had that game won and bad decisions at the end cost us the game," Thompson said. "There were some things we couldn't control that went wrong, but we didn't close that game out at the end."

Lawson, who took 20 shots, called his play "selfish." By the time the Tar Heels boarded the bus for the trip back to the airport, Williams already knew how he planned to handle the meltdown.

Greivis Vasquez posted the first triple-double ever against UNC. (Photo by Jim Hawkins)

opposite: Ty Lawson scored UNC's last 11 points at Miami. (Photo by Jim Hawkins)

Lawson led Carolina with 24 points at Maryland. (Photo by Jim Hawkins)

EVEN BEFORE GETTING on that bus, players were already dreading the next day's practice. They didn't know exactly what it would involve, but they had suspicions. Running, almost certainly. Lots of defensive drills. Maybe some well-timed screaming and yelling.

Instead, they were locked in a room with a television. On that television was the complete tape from the previous day's debacle. Williams shows his team the full tape of a previous game no more than once per season. It's a tiresome process, and he believes college players learn more effectively when they're given easily digestible snippets of points of emphasis.

This time, though, he wanted to show them how they had built their lead, and then how they had frittered it away. He wanted them to be as perplexed at the late-game clock management as he was.

"We showed them every single play," Williams said. "We wanted them to see what we were talking about. For us to spend that much time on that game and go over how poorly we played, I think the kids took that to heart."

They weren't given a choice. After the film session, the Tar Heels hit the court. Close observers of Williams's career will tell you that his practices have mellowed, that he's learned how to taper practices in the second half of the season to ensure his team is fresh on game day. This time, though, there was no tapering.

"Coach thought we were getting a little spoiled," Joe Holladay said. "So we practiced harder. On the outside, everybody thinks practice is blood and guts and diving on the floor and screaming, but it's not. And our guys appreciate that, because they talk to their friends at other schools and they know other places are having 6:00 A.M. practices. So they know Coach will take care of them for the most part, and that's why they play hard on game night.

"The assistants are always trying to get him to practice the kids harder. And after that Maryland game, we did that. And that snapped their attention back."

"We were extremely disappointed about the competitiveness and savvy of our team at the end," Williams said. "We were going to make darn sure we pushed them as much as we could."

That meant pushing them physically as well as asking for more emotionally. Since Lawson's arrival on campus as a freshman, the coaching staff had repeatedly told him that a great Carolina point guard was more than just a

scorer or passer. He was also an on- and off-court leader, the player who knew when more defensive intensity was needed without being told. Like a football quarterback, they told him, the point guard would get too much credit after a victory and definitely too much blame after a loss.

Now, they wanted to add even more duties to Lawson's job description.

"You have to manage the game during crunch time," Steve Robinson told him. "You have to make sure we are taking good shots, and you have to take care of the ball."

"You are the guy we want taking care of the ball at the end," Williams added. "You have to be a facilitator."

CHAPTER TEN

Winning Ugly

When the news broke in August that Marcus Ginyard would miss the early part of the 2008–09 season, an unlikely candidate claimed to be ready to shoulder Ginyard's burden of guarding the opposition's best perimeter player.

"I would like to be that guy," said Wayne Ellington. "I've worked on it, and I'm excited about it. I want to guard the other team's best perimeter player and I want to be able to stop him."

The Tar Heel backcourt's success was uneven at replacing Ginyard's defense. Five different opposing guards had scored at least 30 points against Carolina by late February. After a 104–74 thrashing of outmanned Georgia Tech, another perimeter player with high-scoring potential was next on the schedule.

The March 4 trip to Virginia Tech exemplified everything that makes the Atlantic Coast Conference the best basketball league in America. The Hokies don't have much of a national reputation or get the nation's best recruits, but they play with the same hard edge exhibited by their head coach, Seth Greenberg. Their gym, Cassell Coliseum, is a true "gym" in every good sense of the word: it is not too big, it consistently sells out when the national powers come to town, and it boasts a boisterous student section.

The Tar Heels were arguably in a no-win situation, because no matter what happened in Blacksburg, they still had to defeat Duke in the regular season finale to claim the outright ACC regular season title. Already, most of the talk in Chapel Hill was about Senior Day for one of the most beloved Carolina classes ever.

What worried Roy Williams the most about the Hokies was the fact that they were desperate. At 17–11 overall and 7–7 in the ACC, Virginia Tech was in the familiar late-season position of needing a marquee win to serve as the foundation for their NCAA Tournament credentials. Greenberg had already begun to campaign through the media, and one more victory would have clinched at least a .500 ACC record and made his case much stronger. It was

opposite: Carolina
won six ACC road
games. (Photo by
Jim Hawkins)

the final home game for a Hokie senior class that included standout forward A.D. Vassallo.

"It's hard to beat people on Senior Day," Williams said. "They were fighting for their lives to make the tournament, and we already knew we were going to make the tournament. We knew even if we lost we could still get the ACC title by beating Duke in the last game. So everything psychologically was in their favor except for our toughness."

To emphasize that toughness, Williams made it one of his pregame points. Before his team took the floor, he wrote, "Are we tough enough?" on the board.

Virginia Tech had experienced surprising success against Carolina since joining the league, including a stunning win at the Smith Center during the 2006–07 season. They did it because they usually had at least one guard, sometimes two, capable of breaking down a defense off the dribble and creating his own offense. This year, that guard was Malcolm Delaney, who had already scored 24 points against Virginia, 29 at Miami, 37 against Clemson, and 25 against Florida State. He also had playmaking responsibilities, so the ball spent a lot of time in his hands. Simply denying him the ball was not an option.

Assistant coach C.B. McGrath prepared the Virginia Tech scouting report and delivered these words of wisdom to the Carolina perimeter defenders, and to Ellington specifically: be there on the catch. If Delaney was allowed to catch the ball with no interference, he was likely to drop in a three-pointer or penetrate into the lane and draw a foul.

Right from the beginning, Ellington was Delaney's shadow. He forced an errant three-pointer early in the game and then thwarted a drive to the hoop that ended with an off-balance miss. The first Hokie turnover of the game came when Ellington followed Delaney around two very solid screens, including a solid hip check from Hank Thorns, and knocked the ball free on the wing.

He stayed low going around screens, he always had a hand in his man's face, and he gave minimal help in the post to avoid leaving Delaney free for a perimeter jumper.

"I knew I couldn't get behind those screens," Ellington said. "You have to work. You make sure you shadow him."

Carolina blocked nine Virginia Tech shots in the 86–78 victory. (Photo by Jim Hawkins)

opposite: Ed Davis had eight points and six blocks at Virginia Tech. (Photo by Jim Hawkins)

Ty Lawson scored 16 second-half points in Blacksburg. (Photo by J. D. Lyon Jr.)

opposite: UNC's win clinched a share of the ACC title. (Photo by J. D. Lyon Jr.)

Ellington went to the bench for the first time at the 12:46 mark, and at that point Delaney was scoreless and Carolina had built a 17–8 lead. He made his first and only field goal of the half with 2:27 left, ending the first 20 minutes 1-of-6 from the field.

In the Carolina locker room at halftime, acknowledged defensive leader Bobby Frasor took Ellington aside. "That," Frasor said, "was a great half."

"I thought I had done a pretty good job," Ellington said. "He didn't get any open looks. I wanted to continue that effort in the second half."

He did. He got caught in traffic and allowed Delaney to make a layup three minutes into the half, but that was essentially one of just two defensive mistakes he made the entire game—the other coming when he fell back on his heels and had to swipe and commit a foul as Delaney drove to the hoop.

Delaney finished 4-of-16 and scored 11 of his 19 points in the final 2:41, when he was being guarded by Ty Lawson, who fouled him three of the final four possessions and four of the last six. The Hokies got as close as 63–62 with 5:16 remaining, but Tyler Hansbrough—who contributed 22 points and 15 rebounds—sparked a 10–0 run that led to an 86–78 victory.

"We were sick of people criticizing our perimeter for not being able to guard guys," Ellington said. "That was my emphasis. I didn't want to let him get any open looks. He came off a lot of screens, and I wanted to be there every time he caught the ball. Coach always says, 'Guard people the way you don't want to be guarded.' And I know when I come off screens and guys are right there, it's something I hate."

"I love for us to win in the 90s," Williams said. "I love for it to be pretty and for us to fly up and down the court. But to have a great year, you've got to win some ugly. That was a grind-it-out game, and that made it feel good for me."

Senior Day

In August, Williams had already identified the season finale against Duke as "probably the toughest ticket in Carolina history." In March, he didn't feel any differently about it.

For years, the head coach had counted the 1997 Senior Day game at Kansas as the most emotional of his coaching career. That senior class included Jerod Haase, Scot Pollard, B. J. Williams, and Jacque Vaughn, a group that was extremely close to Williams. But their Senior Day opponent was middling Kansas State, and the Jayhawks were already well on the way to a conference title. Kansas prevailed easily, 78–58.

Twelve years later, that game was finally supplanted.

"This year was far tougher," Williams said of the emotional nature of the final home game for the 2009 seniors. It had all the ingredients of a classic showdown. Rival Duke was in town, with Mike Krzyzewski certainly remembering the way the same basic group of Tar Heels had spoiled a very similar Senior Day for Duke in 2006. A win would give the Tar Heels the outright ACC regular season title. A win also would likely cement a top national seed and a favorable placement in Greensboro for the opening two rounds of the NCAA Tournament. Most important to Williams, however, it was the final home game for a very meaningful senior class and the last time Tyler Hansbrough would play at the Smith Center. For a self-described corny coach who has won every Senior Day game in his career, it was almost unthinkable to imagine sending a treasured group of seniors out with a loss in a game with so much at stake.

"I couldn't sleep for a couple days leading up to it," Williams said. "Everything was lined up against us. I'm one of those corny guys that thinks things should happen just because it's the right thing. I thought it was the right thing for this senior class to win their last home game."

Williams's routine is to eat the pregame meal with his team four hours before tip-off and then take a quick nap. This time, for the first time all sea-

opposite: Tyler Hansbrough's Smith Center salute. (Photo by Jeffrey A. Camarati)

108

son, he couldn't go to sleep. There was too much churning in his head; he was worried about the mechanics of the pregame ceremony, the emotion of his seniors, and the status of his starting point guard.

At Friday's practice, Lawson had banged his big toe into the basket support while running through a drill. The health of that toe would become one of the biggest story lines surrounding Tar Heel hoops through the next month. Lawson didn't come out with the team for early warmups, sending a ripple of concern through the early Smith Center arrivals. Those diehards didn't know that Williams was also concerned; as a firm believer in the importance of getting loose before a game, he wanted his point guard on the floor for warmups.

Instead, Lawson was sequestered in the training room with three nervous athletic-department staffers standing outside the door. At that moment, they were physically closer to Lawson than anyone else, yet they still had absolutely no idea if he would play.

Other than the toe drama, most of the attention that day had been on the core group of seniors. Unexpectedly for a group that had played through dozens of tight situations in their decorated four-year careers, they were also experiencing some butterflies.

Hansbrough had a bevy of family on hand that morning and eventually slipped out, alone, to get breakfast and clear his head. Danny Green was thrilled to be able to play in front of his father, who had watched most of Green's standout career on television. Copeland did sleep the night before, but he "woke up this morning with chills" because of his excitement. Even the normally low-key Frasor, who tended to crack most tension with a joke, discovered the day felt different.

"From the moment I woke up, I was so excited," he said. "We didn't have a shootaround that day, but I went down to the Smith Center to shoot anyway because I had so much energy. After that, I just sat around at home. I couldn't sleep, I couldn't do anything, even though it was a beautiful day outside."

The Carolina Basketball office staff spent the day organizing the pregame ceremony. Senior Day had been an important Carolina tradition ever since the Dean Smith era. As a player at Kansas, the future coaching legend hadn't started his last home game. He remembered that slight later as a coach and began a policy of always allowing his seniors to play the first two minutes of their final home game.

Williams absorbed that lesson and expanded on it when he became the head coach at Kansas. In addition to starting his seniors, he also asked them to address the crowd after the game. When he returned to Chapel Hill, he added

CAROLINA BASKETBALL

that additional touch, creating both pregame and postgame festivities for the seniors.

The ceremony altered the usual pregame rhythm. Parents of the seniors were lined up in the home tunnel a half-hour before tip-off, exchanging hand-shakes and hugs and snapping pictures. They had been following their sons around the country for the past four years and in the process had themselves become close friends. Like their children, it was starting to hit them that those relationships would be changing in the very near future.

With the entire team on the court, the seniors were called individually. They grabbed roses for their mothers and exchanged hugs with their parents. Then they had to walk, alone, to midcourt, where the reality of the situation began to hit them.

"When you're announced at the beginning of the game and you hand that rose to your parents and give them a hug, it definitely hits you," Green said. "A lot of guys got emotional at the beginning of the game."

left: Eric Montross greeted Michael Jordan at the Duke game. (Photo by Jeffrey A. Camarati)

right: Danny Green and his dad before the game. (Photo by J. D. Lyon Jr.)

"I wasn't expecting to cry," Frasor said. "But when they were announcing our names and the place was packed with people standing and cheering for us, you get a little choked up. You realize, 'Wow, this is pretty special. This is going to be my last time here.'"

"I almost broke down before the game when they announced my name," Hansbrough said. "There's this, 'I'm ready to play but I'm not really ready to leave,' kind of feeling. I was trying to hold back some tears.

"It's weird, because you put in so many hours of practice in that gym. You grow to have a bond with the building. You have a rough day and you come in late at night by yourself and put some work in and get away from everything. It's like your second house. To realize you're moving on and next year you're going to be far away, it's tough."

Not every senior was moving on. Marcus Ginyard's redshirt meant he would return for the 2009–10 season and his own Senior Day, but his classmates weren't going to let him be left out of the ceremony. After the scholarship seniors were announced, they pointed to Ginyard, who was standing in a suit with the rest of the Tar Heels. They waved him out to midcourt where, as Frasor said, he would always be a member of the class of 2009.

"It was a rush of emotions at that point," Ginyard said. "I had no idea they were going to do that. It was a good time for us to all be out there together. It was a great moment."

Just as the emotions crested, they had to be stuffed away. This was not like a football homecoming game, where there is pregame emotion but the opponent is sometimes the most lightly regarded on the schedule. Basketball is different. It was Senior Day, but it was also Duke—a very capable Duke team that wanted to win a share of the regular season league title.

As Hansbrough walked back to the Carolina bench, he pumped his fist. "That was my way of saying, 'I'm ready to play,'" he said. "I didn't want to wave. I was ready to play."

Making a sudden shift from heart-wrenching emotion to competitive athletics is not easy, even for the head coach. One moment, he was soaking in the emotion of his seniors accepting well-deserved adulation from the crowd; the next, he had to gather his team and prepare them to beat an archrival.

"It's a problem changing your emotions so quickly," Williams said. "When I looked at Tyler's dad, I just about lost it. Then when Danny and his dad hugged and I looked at Danny on the court, I almost lost it again.

"But I've been very lucky in my coaching career. I can go crazy on an official and then calmly turn around and say, 'Okay, here's what we have to do.' My assistant coaches and players have said something about it before. I believe I can get rid of one emotion very quickly and realize what we have to do next."

What the Tar Heels had to do next was beat the seventh-ranked Blue Devils. But first, there would be one final bit of ceremony. Carolina actually had seven seniors—the four scholarship players plus walk-ons Patrick Moody, J.B. Tanner, and Jack Wooten. This presented a problem: how to start the seniors when only five players could be on the court at one time. Although legend has it that Smith once started more than five players and took a technical foul, no record existed of such an occurrence. Luckily, Williams had encountered a similar situation during his Kansas career. But in the frenzy of activity leading up to Senior Day, he had never clarified his plan with the walk-ons.

When Williams wrote the lineup on the board, it included the four seniors plus Lawson, who had been cleared to play. But then Joe Holladay pulled Tanner aside.

"You know what you're doing, right?" Holladay asked.

Tanner gave him a blank look. "Nope," he replied.

"You go on the court like you're going to start," Williams told him right before tip-off. "I'll let the officials know what's going on. Right before tip, they'll wave you off, and you come back over to the sideline."

So eight Tar Heels actually stood on the court as "Jump Around" played from the Smith Center loudspeaker. Green gave one final last shimmy to his signature song. When the walk-ons were ushered back to the bench, Wooten even gave his own unique interpretation of Green's dance.

Once the game began, the first half looked very similar to the first meeting in Durham. Hansbrough swished two early three-pointers, but Duke built a slim 39–38 halftime lead by penetrating and then kicking to Kyle Singler, who scored 15 first-half points.

Lawson did not make a field goal in the first half and appeared limited by his toe injury. In the second half, however, a key strategic change that had evolved since Williams's return to Carolina created more offensive opportunities for the lightning-quick point guard.

"A few years ago, we never screened on the ball," said Holladay. "We started it with Raymond [Felton], and this year it became our offense a lot. If you've got one of the big guys screening on the ball, that means the other one has more room, and it also gives Ty Lawson room to get to the basket.

"It opens up the floor, because we always screen with a big guy. We don't screen wing-to-wing or guard-to-guard. It always seems to revolve around the Duke game because we know we have to take the ball to the goal against them. They're not going to give us free shots and open three-pointers. We did it the first time against them, then we kind of forgot about it, and then from the second Duke game on it became a primary part of our offense."

When he returned home over the previous summer, Lawson's friends in the Washington, D.C., area—a group that includes NBA standout Kevin Durant—had told him that he had been a different player at Carolina than he had been in high school. At Oak Hill Academy, one of the nation's best prep teams, he had been a consistent offensive threat. At Carolina, he sometimes deferred to his talented teammates.

"We want to see the old Ty," they told him. "You're good enough to do the same things at Carolina that you did here."

With more screens to create space for him, the old Ty appeared in the second half against Duke, slashing to the basket and scoring or finding the open man for an easy basket.

With the Tar Heels holding a 70–68 lead with under four minutes remaining, Lawson—who narrowly missed becoming the fourth Carolina player ever to record a triple double, as he notched 13 points, 9 assists, and

8 rebounds—penetrated and kicked to Green for a three-pointer. Two possessions later, he drove past Jon Scheyer for a backbreaking three-point play
with 1:03 left.

"Once I made that shot, I felt like we won the game," Lawson said. "You
could see it in their expressions. They had played great defense, and to give up
a three-point play is a heart-breaker."

Fittingly, a senior clinched the win. Earlier in the half, Frasor had made a
key defensive play when he drew a charge to snuff a 4-on-1 Duke fast break.
With 55 seconds left, he tied up Gerald Henderson to force a jump ball that
gave Carolina possession, leading the raucous Smith Center crowd that included Michael Jordan, Jerry Stackhouse, Larry Brown, Sean May, and Felton
to serenade him with chants of, "Bobby, Bobby, Bobby . . ."

Senior Mike Copeland. (Photo by Jeffrey A. Camarati)

"That was a big-time feeling," Frasor said. "Coach Williams put me in to play defense and to do the right thing. I saw Gerald driving and I got my hands on the ball. It was a little risky, but I felt it was a jump ball and the ref saw the same thing."

It wasn't until Hansbrough was fouled with 29 seconds left that anyone could relax. When he drew the foul from Scheyer, he struck an atypical celebratory pose, ball raised above his head in triumph. He would finish his Tar Heel career averaging 20.1 points and 10.8 rebounds against the Blue Devils—fitting numbers for a player who had tormented Duke as much as anyone in the history of the rivalry.

"We don't like Duke and they don't like us," Hansbrough said. "We may respect them, but we don't like them."

After cutting down the nets to celebrate the regular-season title, each senior addressed the fans, a final farewell to the sellout crowd that stayed in its seats for almost an hour after the game to honor the seniors.

The head coach sat in his usual spot on the Carolina bench to absorb all the festivities. It was only then, after all the day's events were nearly finished, that he realized how much pressure he had felt during the game.

"I was totally spent," Williams said. "I don't know that I've ever been as emotionally drained as I was at the end of that day. I just wanted those kids to win. I wanted that senior class to go out by winning their last home game. I wanted to see them cut down the nets and be able to see the looks on their faces."

Earning Respect

Ty Lawson played 105 games as a Tar Heel, but it wasn't until his 100th game that Carolina fans and college-basketball observers truly believed in his commitment to winning. Although he had led the team to a pair of ACC Tournament titles his first two years and even hit a critical three-pointer against Louisville to send the Tar Heels to the 2008 Final Four, it wasn't until the final game he would ever play in the Smith Center that people really felt, deep down, that he cared about winning.

Not that anyone disliked him, but most people, including some around the Carolina Basketball family, wondered if Lawson would fight through adversity and put the name on the front of the jersey ahead of his name on the back. People thought he was immature, perhaps not very responsible, but all in all a fun-loving, nice guy with a killer crossover and speed to burn.

The point guard from Clinton, Maryland, had returned to Carolina for his junior season after a much-publicized and debated dalliance with the NBA Draft. Still, questions remained. Lawson himself said NBA scouts challenged his toughness, and others wondered about his motivation: would he be out to showcase his own game, or would he be the throttle in a team attack that was expected to challenge for a national championship?

He missed seven games due to injuries as a sophomore, including the home game against Duke, and there were whispers about his being soft. And he played one of his poorest games against Kansas in the 2008 semifinals, when he had two field goals and two assists and was unable to keep the Jayhawks from thrashing the Tar Heels by 18 points.

Those perceptions all changed in a four-week span beginning March 8, 2009.

Lawson had shown flashes of greatness all season: Most Valuable Player honors in Maui after dismantling eighth-ranked Notre Dame with 22 points and 11 assists; a near-flawless performance in December in the 35-point win at Big Ten favorite Michigan State, in which he had 17 points, eight assists, zero turnovers, and seven steals; a game-winning, buzzer-beating dash and three-pointer at Florida State; a stunning 21-point second-half effort at Duke; and clutch, in-your-face three-pointers in the final minutes of a hard-fought win at Miami.

He was already well on his way to ACC Player of the Year honors, something

Ty Lawson was the second Tar Heel point guard in five years to win MVP honors at the Maui Invitational. (Photo by Jim Hawkins)

no point guard had done in 31 years. He likely had secured a first-round spot in the NBA Draft and was rewriting the ACC record book for assist-turnover ratio. Still, there were doubts about what really fueled Ty Lawson.

Then it happened. In practice on March 6, two days before the second Duke game—one of the most highly anticipated meetings in years—Lawson slammed his right toe into the basket stanchion. Off he went on crutches to student health; turf toe was the diagnosis, a painful injury that typically takes weeks of rest to overcome. The "Ty Lawson Big Toe Watch" officially began.

For the next two days, everyone wondered if he would play, including Roy Williams, Lawson, and all the other players. In practice on Saturday, his toe was so sore that he could barely get the ball to the rim from the free-throw line, prompting the CBS crew watching to issue a network report that put him as questionable.

Williams was skeptical right up until 15 minutes before tip-off. Lawson had come out unusually early to test his foot, then said, "I don't know if I can go because it hurts really bad," as he left the floor with 29 minutes on the pregame clock. He stayed with athletic trainer Chris Hirth to get final treatments, including a shot to numb the pain. Lawson finally returned to the floor with only about 30 seconds left for him to warm up before the court was cleared for Senior Day ceremonies.

Williams was livid. "I got really mad because how can a kid play if he can't warm up and loosen his toe up? He stayed in the trainer's room so dadgum long I didn't even know if he was going to get a warm-up. But he was able to get going.

In the first half, he didn't play very well. He wasn't bad, but things just didn't happen for him. But he got it loose and in the second half he played as well as any point guard I've ever had."

Lawson didn't make a field goal in the first half, although he had five assists as Duke built a 39–38 lead. But just as he had at Cameron Indoor Stadium 25 days earlier, Lawson took over the final 20 minutes, notching 13 points, five rebounds, and four assists and perpetuating the belief that as long as he was on the floor, Carolina was going to win. His three-point play with 1:03 left sealed the victory.

"There was so much emotion that day," said Lawson. "It was Senior Day and we wanted them to go out right. That game was tough, playing with four toes because I could not feel my fifth one. To make that shot and bring the team together, it just felt great."

Lawson helped the Tar Heels clinch outright the regular-season ACC title and gain a likely number-one seed in the NCAA Tournament, and he put a stranglehold on ACC Player of the Year honors. More important, he showed everyone how badly he wanted to win.

"I tell Ty he likes to milk injuries, he's soft—I kind of poke fun at him," said Bobby Frasor. "But then he takes the shot, goes out there and just absolutely dominates and performs as the same Ty he has been all year—that was pretty special."

Tyler Hansbrough said he gained a new level of respect for Lawson that afternoon. "That's when I talk about Ty maturing as a player. He was tougher this year, stronger, competitive, and he wanted to win. He wanted to beat Duke about as much as anybody else, and he 'cowboyed up,' as I like to call it."

But the Duke game only put a temporary muzzle on the questions of his toughness. He was unable to play in the ACC Tournament and the first round of the NCAA Tournament. One national columnist openly questioned his commitment to his teammates.

Such talk was permanently silenced after Lawson's remarkable second half against LSU in Greensboro in the second round. He made the decision to play about 15 minutes before pregame introductions, but this time there would be no anesthesia to deal with the pain—Williams would not permit it.

"I want to win another national championship more than I can breathe, but I am not going to allow that youngster to take another shot," Williams told his staff the week before the NCAA Tournament began.

"I wanted to," said Lawson, "but Coach didn't want to jeopardize my health or injure my foot worse than what it already was. Coach is so selfless. Even though he wanted to win another championship so bad, he looked out for my health and well-being. It speaks volumes to what type of person he is."

Lawson had two points in the first half, overcame a scare when he heard scar tissue pop, and led UNC to a 38–29 lead at intermission. But the Tigers roared out of the blocks in the second half, building a five-point lead with 12:25 to play.

In what turned out to be the only second-half comeback needed in Carolina's national-championship run, Lawson scored 21 points and finished the 84–70 win with six assists and no turnovers. He made one big play after another in the second half: two three-pointers in the first five minutes to keep UNC close; a steal, a driving layup, and a free throw to give the Tar Heels the lead for good with 7:41 to play; and a jaw-dropping crossover drive for a basket with 5:46 to play that would be the signature play of Carolina's postseason run.

It was an epic performance under pressure that would put to rest forever in the hearts and minds of Carolina Nation the toughness and desire to win of Tywon Ronell Lawson.

"I tell our kids all the time, we get a chance to perform on the biggest stage there is, whether it's North Carolina–Duke, the ACC Tournament, the Final Four, or the national championship game," said Williams. "People are going to remember how you played on the biggest stage . . . [and] Ty was not afraid."

"We needed him against LSU, there was no question about that," said backcourt mate Wayne Ellington. "For him to come back and show that type of toughness, that was huge not only for our team, but for himself. People were taking shots at him and questioning his toughness, and the LSU game put all those questions to rest."

Even Frasor was impressed: "The Duke and LSU games really made me raise my eyebrows. The LSU game—his toe isn't 100 percent but he has that second half when he scores 21 points and is just making unbelievable plays; the crossover and the finish in the lane, getting fouled and one. It was one of the best performances I've ever seen."

Jerod Haase said Lawson's ascension to Tar Heel basketball royalty began off the court and then translated to his position as floor leader. "Ty's grown up in a lot of ways. He's matured for three years, whether it's going to class or showing up on time or doing what Coach Williams asks him to do. He's more reliable. The guys understood that, and they saw his competitive desire and the willingness to play through some pain and get out there for the team. He earned a lot of respect from the staff and the players."

Lawson then earned Most Outstanding Player honors at the South Regional in Memphis, becoming the first Tar Heel point guard to ever win that award. He averaged 19 points, seven assists, and just one turnover in the wins over Gonzaga and Oklahoma.

As Carolina advanced to Detroit for the Final Four, Lawson had emerged as the nation's most valuable and unstoppable player. The Tar Heels decidedly beat Villanova and Michigan State, with Lawson orchestrating a devastating attack on both ends of the floor. He had 22 points and eight assists in the semifinal and was presented the Bob Cousy Award as the best point guard in the country on the morning of the title game. Later that evening, he validated the selection with 21 points, six assists, and a championship-game-record eight steals against the Spartans. He made more free throws than any player in Final Four history.

Again, as he had done in Greensboro and Memphis, every time Carolina needed a play to extend the lead or fend off an opponent's rally, Lawson was the man to make that play.

"Ty's play was the finest I have seen by a point guard throughout an NCAA Tournament since Indiana's Isiah Thomas in 1981," said Williams.

Lawson averaged 20.8 points and had 34 assists, 16 steals, and only seven turnovers in his five postseason games.

"What he showed us in that last month was that he was 100 percent committed to doing everything he needed to do for this team to succeed," said Marcus Ginyard. "That's something

Ty Lawson set the ACC single-season record for assist-error ratio. (Photo by Todd Melet)

Ty Lawson kept everyone relaxed, even at the pre-Duke press conference. (Photo by Bob Leverone, *The Sporting News*)

everybody outside this program has questioned—his commitment to the team first. There's no doubt he answered all those questions."

"I usually don't show too much emotion, and I am a nonchalant player and that is why people think I don't want to win," Lawson said. "I really wanted to win this tournament, and that is why I came back to school. I wanted to be the last one standing. I want people to remember me as a goofy player off the court who loved to have fun. But on the court I am a serious player. I would do anything to make my team win."

Let there be no doubt about who Ty Lawson is. National champion. ACC Player of the Year. Top point guard in the country. And, yes, one of the best big-time competitors to ever play for the Tar Heels.

CHAPTER TWELVE

Postseason

Once it became obvious that Ty Lawson wouldn't play in the ACC Tournament, expectations had to be adjusted. It was generally accepted that no matter what happened, Carolina had already wrapped up a top seed in the forthcoming NCAA Tournament. The league had moved the event to Atlanta's Georgia Dome, a swap that, when combined with the struggling economy, removed the casual fan from the tournament. In a building where nearly twice as many had filled the seats eight years earlier, only 26,352—still an impressive total, but one that left gaping empty sections of seats in the upper level—showed up for Carolina's first-round game against Virginia Tech.

Players and coaches alike realized that no matter what happened at the Georgia Dome, whether it was a third straight tournament title or an early first-round exit, it would be mostly forgotten by the time the NCAA brackets were released on Sunday evening. Roy Williams might have originally been drawn to engineering as a student, but he also understood history. He knew that when he made the annual Rams Club circuit in April 2008, there weren't many fans who wanted to chat about the ACC Tournament championship; quite a few wanted to hear about the Kansas loss in the Final Four.

But Williams is also a man who will turn anything into a competition, including throwing a balled-up piece of scrap paper into the trash can in his office. Fans sometimes misinterpreted his comment, "We're going to play in it, and we're going to try and win the sucker," as indifference. It was exactly the opposite. Sure, he probably wouldn't have chosen to pack up his team and haul them to Atlanta when he would've rather been wrapping Lawson in bubble wrap and preparing for the NCAA Tournament. But once they turned on the Georgia Dome lights and quarterfinal opponent Virginia Tech ran out of the tunnel, he felt the same competitive burn that he feels for every other game.

That mood translated to his team. Wayne Ellington was superb, with a stat-stuffing line of 16 points, five rebounds, and four assists. Tyler Hansbrough

"When a man is tapped on the shoulder, what a tragedy it would be if he was unprepared for his finest hour."

Thought for the Day, March 17, 2009

showed as much emotion on the court as he had at any time in his Carolina career, pumping his fist after big baskets, exhorting his teammates to make important defensive stops, and exchanging a sternum-shaking chest bump with Deon Thompson. And the wily coach, the one who supposedly didn't care about the "cocktail party," masterfully orchestrated the game's final minute as the Tar Heels torpedoed Virginia Tech's NCAA chances for the second time in 10 days and handed them a painful ACC elimination for the second straight season (a year earlier, Hansbrough had nailed a buzzer-beating jump shot and then celebrated with an arms-flailing dash down the court).

This time, the Hokies again had a late lead, as A.D. Vassallo made a layup with 52 seconds left to give his team a 76–75 lead. Hansbrough answered 20 seconds later with a field goal of his own, putting the Tar Heels back in front. That's when coaching took over. Carolina had just three team fouls, giving them the ability to defend aggressively without concern of giving up free throws on nonshooting fouls. Ellington committed the team's fourth foul with 22 seconds left, and Hansbrough fouled six seconds later.

Virginia Tech had the opportunity to make the game's final shot, but Hansbrough reached in for a jump ball on J.T. Thompson with 5.2 seconds left that gave alternating possession to the Tar Heels. While Seth Greenberg was flinging off his jacket in disgust—"I guess we foul and they don't," he would say sarcastically after the game—Williams was preparing to channel Dean Smith by making 5.2 seconds last closer to 10 minutes.

Carolina had to inbound the ball under the Hokie basket, a dangerous spot. So Williams called a time-out.

"First, he told us to get the ball in safely," said Thompson. "But he also told us we had another time-out if we needed it, and not to force a pass."

"He set up a play for us," Ellington said. "We weren't just trying to get the ball inbounds, we were trying to get it to one of our good free-throw shooters."

Following the time-out, the ball went to Hansbrough, who had already made all eight of his charity tosses. He made two more, giving him 28 points for the afternoon. There were 4.6 seconds left, and Williams called another time-out.

"We have fouls to give," the coach reminded his team. With just five team fouls and a three-point lead, one foul could be given before putting the Hokies in the one-and-one. Williams reminded his team to foul on the dribble rather than the shot, meaning he didn't want to risk fouling a Virginia Tech three-point shooter, which would have given the Hokies three free throws. Tech inbounded the ball in the backcourt, and Thompson fouled almost immediately.

Danny Green made just three shots in the ACC Tournament. (Photo by Robert Crawford)

opposite: Ed Davis contributed key minutes in Atlanta. (Photo by Kevin Cox, Getty Images)

There were 3.5 seconds left, and Williams called another time-out, his third in less than two seconds.

Now his team was squarely in the middle of one of the most oft-debated scenarios in college hoops: with a three-point lead on the game's last possession, is it preferable to foul and never give the opponent the opportunity to shoot a three-pointer, or should the leading team play good defense and contest the three-pointer?

Williams chose the former. "We wanted to foul coming out of the time-out," Ellington said. "We wanted to foul on the dribble."

That was the one part of the endgame that didn't go according to the head coach's plan, as Vassallo hoisted a three-pointer before contact could be made. Per his instructions, however, his team did not foul on the shot, and Vassallo's last-gasp attempt bounced off the rim. Carolina survived, and Hansbrough sprinted off the court and into a Georgia Dome tunnel — one that led nowhere; it was a dead end. In his excitement, he had run the wrong way.

"Everybody was laughing about that," Hansbrough said.

They weren't laughing about the way they'd outwitted the Hokies, having once again beaten them at a time when the opponent had everything to gain. The final 5.2 seconds had been a coaching clinic — not just in the art of extending a game, but in explaining why sometimes time-outs are better used late in the game rather than early.

"At the end of the game, that's when you need those time-outs," said Tyler Zeller. "You make one mistake that leads to a layup, and those two points can cost you the game. So you have to be very detailed on every possession and make sure everyone understands exactly what is happening. That's the value of a time-out."

Even after a semifinal loss to an inspired Florida State squad, the Tar Heels were also reminded of the value of depth. With Lawson out, the point guard load had fallen to senior Bobby Frasor and freshman Larry Drew II. Although they didn't score like Lawson, they had managed the offense and defense very effectively. Drew II posted seven assists against just two turnovers in Atlanta, while Frasor played all but 10 minutes in the two games.

Bobby Frasor started both ACC Tournament games. (Photo by Robert Crawford)

opposite: Bobby Frasor made his first NCAA start since 2006. (Photo by Bob Rosato, *Sports Illustrated*)

In fact, as the Tar Heels left the Georgia Dome, the point guard position was not at the top of the list of concerns. Instead, it was the play of Danny Green, who shot just 3-for-25 in Atlanta and uncharacteristically missed three straight layups against the Seminoles.

In the postgame locker room, Joe Holladay walked up to the visibly disappointed Green.

"I'm not worried about you," Holladay told him. "We've got some big games left. And you've got some big games left."

Green nodded. Less than 36 hours later, he and his teammates would learn their first-round NCAA assignment: a date with Radford in Greensboro.

IN THE WAKE of the ACC Tournament performance, Roy Williams met with Frasor, who would be the team's starting point guard for one more game. Already, the weekend off was providing Lawson with some encouraging signs, but he wasn't yet ready to play.

"Looking back on it, not playing was a great decision," Lawson said. "If I had played in the ACC Tournament, I probably would have missed the first two or three games in the NCAA Tournament."

Instead, he would only miss the opener against the Highlanders. But after the Tar Heels had turned in back-to-back, sub-80-point games in the ACC Tournament—the only time all season that would happen—Williams wanted to make sure Frasor knew the head coach still expected a brisk tempo even without the regular starter.

The two shared a unique bond. Williams respected Frasor's savvy as the son of a coach, and Frasor had endeared himself to the Tar Heel head coach by running the team as a freshman during the remarkable 2005–06 campaign. That season was one of Williams's favorites as a head coach, as his teams rarely had the opportunity to be true underdogs. That squad had shattered every expectation, and Frasor was largely the architect of the team.

Now a senior, Frasor didn't have the same raw foot speed as Lawson, but experience had taught him the ball could move just as fast, if not faster, via the pass rather than the dribble.

"It's a weird feeling, because I know Ty gives us the best chance to win any game, because he's one of the best point guards in the country," Frasor said. "But at the same time, I was like, 'I can still play this game. We won a lot

left: Ty Lawson was unable to play in the ACC Tournament due to a jammed toe on his right foot. (Photo by Robert Crawford)

right: Tyler Hansbrough set the ACC scoring record with this free throw against Radford. (Photo by J. D. Lyon Jr.)

of games with me playing point guard.' So in the Radford game, I wanted to show that we could still push the ball. I don't have the same end-to-end speed as Ty, but I can still pitch the ball ahead and throw the pass to a big guy for an easy layup."

Even without Lawson, the Tar Heels seemed energized by having finally arrived at the point of the season they'd been waiting for since April 2008. This was the atmosphere Lawson, Ellington, and Green had anticipated. This was the win-or-go-home pressure they'd wanted.

Now, they had a chance to act on it.

"We waited so long to get back to the NCAA Tournament and redeem ourselves," Ellington said. "When we got there, everyone took it as a businesslike approach. We didn't go anywhere to have fun and we didn't go anywhere to go sightseeing. We were there for business."

There were plenty of smiles as Carolina beat Radford, 101–58, in the first round of the NCAA Tournament. (Photo by Streeter Lecka, Getty Images)

All season, Holladay had pointedly worn his 2005 national championship ring. He'd make sure it was visible to the players, and in case they missed the implication, he'd sometimes wave it in front of their faces. The 2005 team had made it a crusade to reach the Final Four so Steve Robinson would stop wearing his Kansas shirt from the 2003 Final Four. The 2009 team wanted their own ring to force Holladay to wear some new jewelry.

The detonation when the Tar Heels finally played an NCAA Tournament game was impressive. Hansbrough became the ACC's all-time leading scorer early in the first half—fittingly, he did it on a free throw—but the story of the day was the offensive onslaught that drowned Radford in a flurry of open shots. Carolina forced 18 turnovers, and Frasor continuously pushed the ball ahead to create 25 fast-break points, resulting in a 101–58 thrashing that was the program's second-largest NCAA win of all time.

Green returned to form with a double-double, and Ellington shot 11-for-16 while also finding time to grab eight rebounds. The Tar Heels had done more than just survive a late-season injury to a key player, every coach's darkest fear. They had thrived.

Building a Friendship, Finding a Place

Although they attended high schools 3,000 miles apart and barely knew each other before enrolling at Carolina, Ed Davis and Larry Drew II bonded quickly.

Soon after they moved in with fellow freshmen Tyler Zeller and Justin Watts to a dormitory suite near the Smith Center, the pair developed a tight relationship more akin to brothers than unfamiliar roommates.

They bickered and needled one another endlessly about video games, basketball, and cleaning the kitchen in settings ranging from their dorm and the locker room to locales around the country.

It was no different atop Maui's Black Rock near the UNC team hotel in November, when Drew II prodded Davis into leaping off the 40-foot cliff into the Pacific Ocean.

"I think Ed's always trying to beat me, always trying to compete with me for stuff, but I don't know why," Drew II said. "That's just the way Ed is—he's always trying to outdo me for some reason."

The quick friends may have found common ground in their shared backgrounds. Both are sons of 10-year NBA veterans and played the game since they could first hold a basketball as a toddler.

After a broken wrist sidelined Zeller for most of the season, Davis and Drew II became the primary new contributors for head coach Roy Williams on the court, while Watts helped more behind the scenes as a freshman member of the Blue Team.

The adjustment wasn't always easy. Drew II was a backup to eventual ACC Player of the Year Ty Lawson.

"The coaches were telling me to focus on pushing the ball," Drew II remembered. "Even when I thought I was pushing it as fast as I could go, they told me I looked like I was going 60 or 70 percent. I thought, 'This is as fast as I can go!' The speed at which they want you to play is incredible, but it really pays off at the end."

Davis was trying to crack a rotation of big men that included a returning starter in Deon Thompson and a returning National Player of the Year in Tyler Hansbrough.

"Coming here, all I wanted to do was win," Davis said. "I never thought about how many minutes I was going to get per game. I just thought about it in the back of my mind that when I got in the game, at least there is something I can try to do to change the game around. Just block a shot or get a tough rebound, or an offensive rebound."

Davis was a quick study in the paint, grabbing a team-high 14 rebounds and scoring 10 points for a double-double against Penn in his first college game. He had nine points and 10 boards in 23 minutes against Kentucky in his second game and posted two more double-doubles before the end of November.

Drew II tallied similarly impressive numbers behind Lawson early in the season, amassing seven assists and three steals against Chaminade and five more assists against Oregon in Maui. He added six more assists in Chapel Hill against UNC Asheville on November 30.

As 2008 nonconference games turned to 2009 ACC games, Drew II's minutes on the court were sporadic. He played less than 10 minutes in 13 of 17 games between January 1 and the end of the regular season.

"This whole style of play takes time, especially at the point guard position," Drew II said. "I played well at the beginning and did hit a rough spot, but I just tried to learn from my mistakes."

Meanwhile, Davis grew accustomed to being the first man off the Carolina bench in most games. He didn't reach double figures in points between December 3 and March 13, but his season average of one rebound every 2.9 minutes played was among the highest in UNC history. Davis averaged 6.7 points, 6.6 rebounds, and 1.7 blocked shots per game for the season, earning a spot on the ACC's All-Freshman Team after leading the team in blocked shots and finishing second in rebounding.

"Getting all the experience from the preseason to

Larry Drew II had three points and seven assists versus Chaminade. (Photo by J. D. Lyon Jr.)

Ed Davis played his best basketball in March. (Photo by Bob Donnan)

the ACC, the game just becomes easier and it slows down," Davis said. "At the end of the season, . . . the small things Coach was preaching the whole year were just starting to pay off."

After a toe injury to Lawson necessitated increased playing time for Drew II in early March, the freshman saw his chance to make up for his rough January and February.

"I have to get into a rhythm when I play," he said. "It was tough playing two or three minutes then resting. I think it was the most difficult thing for me coming in transitionwise, learning how to play off the bench."

Drew II backed up Bobby Frasor, Lawson's replacement in the starting lineup, in both ACC Tournament games, dishing out seven assists against just two turnovers in 31 minutes of consistent action. In the eight postseason games of ACC and NCAA Tournament play, Drew II had 13 assists and three turnovers in 72 minutes.

"It was definitely the silver lining to losing in the ACC Tournament," Frasor said. "Larry, Ed, and I all got big-time minutes in those two games. Larry showed some glimpses of brilliance while making some great assists and controlling the tempo of the game."

After quickly coming together off the court as roommates, then seeing their minutes on the court diverge during the season, Davis and Drew II spent more time together on the floor in the postseason. The point guard played as well as he had in months, and the big man suddenly became a force on both ends of the court.

Davis scored a season-high 15 points in the NCAA first-round game against Radford and had nine points and seven rebounds two days later against LSU as Carolina advanced to the Sweet 16. The NCAA championship game against Michigan State was Davis's breakthrough performance nationally, recording 11 points and eight boards in just 14 minutes against the Spartans.

Fans can expect even more friendly bickering behind the scenes in 2009–10, as Drew II and Davis room together again and see increased roles on a re-vamped Tar Heel squad.

CHAPTER THIRTEEN

Senior Motivation

"Survive and advance."

Thought for the Day, March 20, 2009

Every road to the national championship contains that one unexpected regional road bump. The 1982 Tar Heels had to sweat it out against James Madison. The '93 squad barely edged Cincinnati. The 2005 team narrowly defeated Villanova.

As it turned out, in 2009 that test would come against Louisiana State, the region's eighth seed. The Tigers were probably underseeded; they were the SEC regular-season champion and boasted the league's player of the year plus two members of the conference's all-defensive team.

But Roy Williams had two reasons to feel confident about the second-round matchup. First, he was getting his point guard back, as Ty Lawson's toe had improved enough to allow him to start. And second, the head coach finally had his fashion choices figured out.

"In 2005, Alexander Julian called me and said, 'I've got a new suit for you, and it's a good-luck suit for the tournament,'" Williams said. "I wore the suit and we won the whole thing. I didn't hear from him before the tournament in 2006, 2007, or 2008.

"This year, before the last Duke game, he calls and says, 'We've got another suit we want you to try.'"

Williams wore the suit for the first time against LSU. Early in the game, it appeared that Julian, one of the nation's most prestigious designers, had forgotten to weave good luck into his signature fabrics. During the first half, Lawson heard a pop in his foot while making a move. He came out of the game almost immediately and took a seat next to trainer Chris Hirth.

"I went over to the bench and I thought I was going to be done for the game," Lawson said. "I really could not walk. It was so painful."

Hirth provided some treatment. After a couple of minutes on the bench, Joe Holladay went to check on the point guard.

"What do you think?" Holladay asked him.

"It hurts more than anything I've ever had in my life," Lawson told him.

opposite: Ed Davis had nine points against LSU. (Photo by Streeter Lecka, Getty Images)

Ty Lawson in pain against LSU. (Photo by Bob Donnan)

"A lot of people would've been down on the end of the bench with their shoe off talking to the trainer," Holladay said later. "But he had made up his mind after the Kansas game that nothing was going to keep him out of those NCAA games. Nothing."

A few moments after leaning back with his hands covering his face in pain, Lawson turned to Holladay. "I can go back in and play," he said.

Although he wasn't particularly effective in the first half, he still helped the Tar Heels build what felt like a secure 38–29 halftime lead.

Maybe it felt too secure. Less than three minutes into the second half, LSU had surged to a 42–41 lead, setting the stage for the most ferociously contested half of the postseason.

"LSU came out real strong in the second half," Lawson said. "I saw the way the game was changing and it reminded me of the [2007] Georgetown game when they came back from a big deficit and knocked down everything. At one point, I got emotional because I did not want to lose. It had a surreal feeling because our season could be over."

With 17:02 remaining in the half and suddenly facing a one-point deficit after a 13–3 LSU run, Williams took a rare early time-out. The time-out surprised some of his players, who were accustomed to his hoarding the valuable commodities until late-game situations. The shock value increased when the team huddled and the point of the stoppage became clear.

Because of television demands, NCAA Tournament time-outs are longer than regular-season time-outs. Usually, the Tar Heels have finished any discussions long before the second horn sounds, and Williams sends his team back on the court by saying, "These time-outs are too freakin' long, I don't have anything else to say."

This time, he had plenty to say.

"He wasn't happy at all," Jack Wooten said. "Coach talked for a good minute and a half, and there was a lot of screaming and yelling, from him and from the rest of the coaches. There wasn't much strategy. It was all motivation and talking about pride."

That motivation took on a pointed edge when directed at the Carolina seniors.

"Do you want your careers to end right now?" he asked Frasor, Hansbrough, and Green. "Do you want the season to end? Because if you keep playing the way you are, that's what is going to happen."

"That hit me right in the stomach," Frasor said.

"Right then, we got hungry," Hansbrough said. "We weren't ready to be done."

LSU actually stretched the lead to 44–41 on a Chris Johnson dunk, but then Lawson nailed his first three-pointer of the game to tie the score. The next 10 minutes were NCAA Tournament basketball at its best, with both sides making repeated big plays. On one side, there was Marcus Thornton throwing in an impossible three-pointer over Green's outstretched arms — "I didn't even think he could get it off, much less make it," Green said. But Ellington and Lawson matched Thornton's every jumper with one of their own.

The intensity on the court trickled over to the bench. With 12:47 left and LSU leading 51–48, Green came back into the game. But he immediately made a mental miscue on the in-bounds play, as he miscommunicated with Frasor. That prompted a predictable rebuke from Williams. Green, who believed he had made the right play, looked miffed at the reprimand. That look prompted Williams to yank him out of the game again, just nine seconds after he had entered it. Miffed at the quick hook, Green tossed his towel over the UNC bench, a rare display of frustration. A few seconds later, the tension dissolved.

"At that point in the season, we were so comfortable with each other that it was easy to talk about it," Green said. "[Coach] came and talked to me and said to forget it and play basketball. He said the team needed me."

Those moments were perhaps the most telling signs of Green's maturation.

"It was an emphasis for me all year not to worry about the bad plays that happen," he said. "I wanted to get back in and try to make some good things happen. I knew there was still time for me to make an impact on the game. I started playing some decent defense, and I got a couple of steals."

While the sideline drama was playing out, Lawson was turning in one of the best point-guard performances in Carolina postseason history. He scored 21 of his 23 points after halftime, and he scored them on a variety of jitterbug, twisting moves that were unex-

Danny Green sank a key second-half three-pointer to help beat LSU. (Photo by Jim Hawkins)

pected from a player who earlier in the game had looked like someone unable to walk.

The signature play came after Thornton had buried back-to-back three-pointers, the kind of offensive explosion that sometimes signals an upset. But Lawson made a steal and out-sprinted two Tigers to the basket, absorbing the contact and converting a three-point play to give Carolina a 67–63 lead.

One minute later, Green fired a dismally off-the-mark three-pointer that thudded off the front rim. But Ellington kept the ball alive, tipping it into the air along the baseline and then throwing it back inbounds, where Green was still standing wide open behind the three-point line. Lawson was open at the top of the key, and an entry pass to Ed Davis or Deon Thompson was available. But this was Green, the king of the quick trigger. Without a pause, he fired again, and this time he made it.

"I focused on the process, on holding my follow through," Green said. "The first one was short and I tried to adjust to make it go in this time."

"When I saw Danny shoot the first one, I went to the glass," Ellington said. "I smacked it to Danny, and I wasn't expecting him to shoot it again. I was like, 'Oh, man.' But he buried it, and it was huge for us and for me emotionally."

The entire play — from Ellington's hustle to Green's willingness to take a risk — was a highlight reel. "That was a legendary play," Frasor said.

On the next possession, Lawson got the ball just left of the top of the key and made a right-to-left crossover move that left three LSU defenders empty-handed. The Tar Heels closed the game on a 20–7 run and won by the deceptive margin of 84–70. After the game, CBS play-by-play man Jim Nantz called Lawson's performance one of the best he had ever seen.

"I think Ty got to the point that he thought he was unguardable," said C.B. McGrath. "We had seen that at times when we played Duke when he was younger, where he would just take it and go with it. This year, you saw it more, where he knew he could take over the game. I think that has a lot to do with confidence and maturity."

"I think that was the best half Ty has ever played," Hans-

Lawson's three-point play gave Carolina the lead for good. (Photo by Bob Donnan)

opposite: Williams wasn't happy with the second-half start. (Photo by Jim Hawkins)

top: Tyler Hansbrough congratulated Lawson for his second-half resurgence. (Photo by Streeter Lecka, Getty Images)

bottom: Wayne Ellington cheered on Danny Green after his three-pointer gave UNC a 70–63 lead. (Photo by Todd Melet)

CBS's Jim Nantz and Lawson.
(Photo by Robert Crawford)

brough said. "It showed how this team has matured, because we realized they couldn't guard Ty."

The score showed another second-round double-digit victory. The players knew better. The head coach gave the entire team the day off the following day—no practice, no tape, no meetings—a rare postseason concession to the type of battle they'd been in against the Tigers.

"I was telling someone the day before that the NCAA games so far had been boring," Frasor said. "There hadn't been any excitement. And then I get to play in a game like this. You grow up watching these games as a kid. To be a part of it, to get to go to the Sweet 16, that's a dream come true."

www.SI.com

MARCH 30, 2009

Sports Illustrated

SWEET SIXTEEN

Let's Get It On

Ty Lawson Leads the Surging Heels

BY TIM LAYDEN

Photo by Bob Rosato, *Sports Illustrated*

An Unsung Hero

Ask Tar Heel fans to identify the most valuable member of the 2008–09 Carolina team and you might get answers ranging from returning National Player of the Year Tyler Hansbrough to ACC Player of the Year Ty Lawson, Final Four Most Outstanding Player Wayne Ellington, or even head coach Roy Williams.

Few fans would cite Chris Hirth, the new athletic trainer who was in his first season replacing longtime trainer Marc Davis, who had retired the previous summer. To those in the Carolina locker room, however, Hirth's worth was never in question.

That the Tar Heels were able to win the 2009 NCAA championship despite injuries that forced Hansbrough, Lawson, Marcus Ginyard, Tyler Zeller, and Mike Copeland to miss a combined 77 games is a testament to Hirth's hard work and talent.

"We all sensed that he was as nervous as he could possibly be, and so I kept telling him I was going to fire him," Williams laughed. "I felt like that would either cure him or get him to turn around and relax. A couple of times I would say, 'Chris, I understand what's going on. Let's just do our best.' I really loved the job he did. I think he was sensational for us. He was very unlucky that some weird things happened that got so much attention and were so important to our team, but he really did a great job."

In Hirth's dizzying first preseason on the bench, the Smith Center training room was typically crowded before and after practice.

Copeland was rehabilitating the anterior cruciate ligament that he tore during a summer pickup game and eventually missed the first 12 games of the season. Ginyard learned in the first week of October that he had a stress fracture in his left foot that required surgery. And the day before Halloween, news spooked Tar Heel fans that a stress reaction in Hansbrough's right shin would sideline him indefinitely. Hansbrough missed the first (and only) four games of his career to start the season.

"It was the strangest thing ever," senior Jack Wooten said. "You look up and we're down to a nine-man rotation, eight-man rotation, when everyone before the season is talking about the deepest team ever with 12, 11 people who can play significant minutes. So you definitely saw it have an impact because the bench got shorter."

Chris Hirth with Tyler Zeller. (Photo by Jim Bounds)

Two games into the young season, more bad news arrived: Zeller broke his left wrist against Kentucky, and doctors described the injury as likely to be season ending.

"I felt bad for Chris, especially when Coach was always joking about him losing his job if somebody else gets hurt," said Ginyard. "I think Chris is the last one to laugh at those jokes, so I get a little nervous for him."

Hirth remembered: "I'll never forget, after the news broke on Tyler Hansbrough's stress reaction, I was sitting there at my desk in the morning and Marc [Davis] said to me, 'You've had more stuff happen to you at this point in the preseason than I've had in the last three to five years. Put it in perspective—it's been a rough start, but it'll get better, things will smooth out.'"

Things eventually did get easier. Hansbrough's stress reaction never developed into a fracture. Copeland returned to action on December 31 at Nevada. Zeller beat the odds and reentered the rotation against NC State on February 18. Ginyard's slow-to-heal foot was a definite disappointment, but after missing 35 games, he successfully applied for a medical redshirt that will allow him to return as a fifth-year senior in 2009–10.

As February turned to March, Hirth's primary concern became Lawson's right big toe, which he jammed on a basket support in practice two days before the home finale against Duke. A painkilling shot helped Lawson pilot the win over the Blue Devils, but he missed both ACC Tournament games and the NCAA opener against Radford.

Lawson's toe became the topic of conversation on ESPN's *SportsCenter* and *Pardon the Interruption* and other talk shows nationwide, even drawing a mention from President Barack Obama when he announced his NCAA bracket picks in March. At a media interview session in Greensboro during the first weekend of NCAA action, Hirth wrapped Lawson's toe while surrounded by more than two dozen reporters and TV cameras.

"I had underestimated the amount of time I had to do his tape job—all of a sudden the doors opened and I still hadn't finished," Hirth said. "Literally, I was surrounded by cameras and lights [and] barely could move. I almost had to fling my elbows out and start swinging my arms to get some positioning in front of him just to finish what I wanted to do. When I did finish, I was able to squeeze my way out. It was intense."

Lawson returned to the lineup in the NCAA second round against LSU, scoring 21 second-half points. He went on to be named MVP of the South Regional, all the while dutifully rehabbing with Hirth to prevent reinjury.

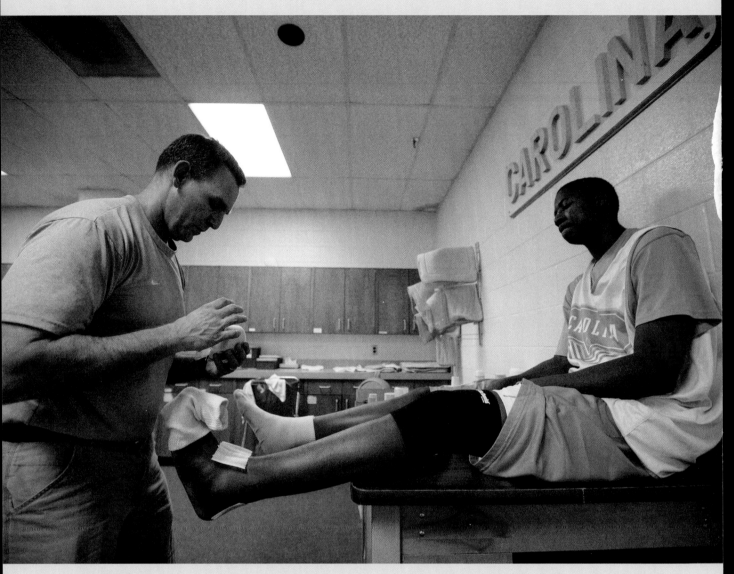

Carolina players spent a lot of time in the athletic training room getting ready for practice. (Photo by Bob Leverone, *The Sporting News*)

"His harping on me to rehab my toe, that's what helped me out a lot," said Lawson. "Without Chris, I would not even know what to do with my toe."

Danny Green and Ed Davis aggravated previous nagging injuries in the Final Four against Villanova, but both worked diligently with Hirth and were able to play in the title-game victory over Michigan State two days later.

"It's really a storybook ending from the way things were expected to be and how they finished out," said Hirth. "It gets better by the day, and I'm really enjoying it."

CHAPTER FOURTEEN

The Duckmaster

"When love and skill work together, expect a masterpiece!"
Thought for the Day, March 24, 2009

Late in the regular season, Bobby Frasor was in the Smith Center writing a paper on a locker-room computer. Tyler Hansbrough was also finishing some homework. It was an entirely normal afternoon—until something completely unexpected happened.

Roy Williams walked into the room. "Hey, do you guys know how to play Guitar Hero?" he asked the two seniors.

Asking Frasor and Hansbrough this question was akin to asking them if they knew how to breathe. Video games are a staple at the house they share with Marcus Ginyard and Danny Green, and Guitar Hero is one of the most popular. The game posted $1 billion in sales in just 26 months, an industry record. It is to the generation of current players what Pac-Man was to the Michael Jordan–Sam Perkins era.

"Can you show me how to play?" Williams asked.

A copy of Guitar Hero is a fixture in the UNC players' lounge, which also happened to boast the guitar accessory the players had pooled their tickets to win in Chicago before Christmas.

"I turned the game on and put it on medium difficulty," Frasor said. "I didn't have him play, because there's no chance he would've known what to do. I played a song for him and he thought it was super interesting."

"Okay, good," Williams said after the brief tutorial. "I need to be better at this than Coach Knight."

That's former Indiana and Texas Tech head coach Bob Knight, perhaps one of the few people on the planet less likely to spend time on video games than Williams. After receiving quizzical looks from Hansbrough and Frasor, Williams explained the situation: he'd been asked to film a commercial for the popular video game. Continuing a series of spots featuring some of the biggest names in sports, the ad would also include Knight, Mike Krzyzewski, and Rick Pitino. The Tar Heel head coach eventually put the matter to his players: was this something he should do? They were enthusiastic, with one small fear.

"Immediately, the *Risky Business* scene came to mind," Frasor said.

Good instincts. All the other Guitar Hero commercials had featured celebrities—major celebrities, like Olympic swimmer Michael Phelps and Lakers star Kobe Bryant—spoofing the Tom Cruise dancing scene from the 1983 film. Odds were good that Williams had been too busy selling calendars out of the back of his car back then to make it to his local cinema, so he had little knowledge of what to expect.

Although they appear together in the final version of the commercial, the four superstar coaches filmed their portions of the advertisement separately on a Raleigh soundstage. As Frasor had guessed, producers wanted Williams to reenact the Cruise scene. In the film, the movie star wears briefs. When Williams arrived on set, he was handed a pair of briefs.

"Hold on," he said. "I think I need to talk to the producer. I'm not wearing these."

But he did dance around in his boxers for the spot, which premiered during the NCAA Tournament. When word first began to trickle out that Carolina's coach was going to shimmy across TV screens in his underwear, the news was greeted with skepticism. Would the Hall of Fame coach really appear on national television without pants?

He would. And that wasn't the only lighthearted moment Williams would enjoy during his team's march to the national title. Upon advancing to the NCAA regionals in Memphis, the Tar Heels were assigned to the historic Peabody Hotel in downtown Memphis. The Peabody featured perhaps the quintessential hotel lobby, stately rooms, and a terrific location within walking distance of the game site, the FedExForum. But it was most famous for its ducks. Williams had stayed at the property on several previous visits but had never taken time to see the ducks.

The tradition began in 1933, when the hotel manager put live ducks in the lobby fountain as a joke. Guests loved it, and in 1940 a hotel bellman offered to take care of the ducks and lead them to and from the lobby each day. The famous Peabody Duck March was born, and the Peabody Duckmaster became one of the most prestigious jobs in Memphis.

Every day at 11:00 A.M., the ducks are taken from their "Duck Palace" on the hotel roof, ride down in the elevator, and march across a red carpet in the lobby to the fountain. At 5:00 P.M., they reverse their path and return to the Duck Palace. Both parts of the trip are greeted with great formality and ceremony, with tourists filling the lobby to snap photos. Throughout the team's stay in Memphis, the Peabody lobby hummed with visitors. In fact, on the morning of the regional final, Oklahoma head coach Jeff Capel was spotted watching the ducks with his family.

Roy Williams's traditional spit in the river. (Photo by J. D. Lyon Jr.)

Where there are tourists with cameras, of course, there are celebrities, and honorary Duckmasters have included Oprah Winfrey, Kevin Bacon, and Emeril Lagasse. Williams joined their ranks the day before the regional semifinal against Gonzaga, as he was given a cane—all Duckmasters have a cane—and the duty of corralling the ducks and sending them to the fountain.

"They take coaching really well," Williams reported with a smile. He was so taken by the experience that he visited the hotel gift shop to purchase a baseball cap with a giant cartoon duck on the front.

For a man who gives up his beloved game of golf during the basketball season, it was a little jarring to find him suddenly experiencing some of the city's

left: Players joined
Williams at the river.
(Photo by J. D. Lyon Jr.)

right: The Tar Heels
visited the National
Civil Rights Museum.
(Photo by J. D. Lyon Jr.)

best tourist activities on the same weekend that his team played for a chance at the Final Four. Part of his more relaxed attitude was a calculated attempt to portray a positive outlook for his team. But part of it was the genuine peace created by the rapport he had built with this experienced group of players.

"We had a lot of adversity this year," Williams said. "If I said, 'Woe is me,' and talked about that all the time, that would get a negative reaction from the players. And I was confident. With me, even when I'm not confident, I try to give the kids the feeling that I am. But I was very confident with this team. We were in a great scenario. We knew those two games in Memphis would be big-time games, and they were. But we came ready to play."

A FEW DRILLS WERE prepractice staples for the Tar Heels all season. The entire roster would always work on shooting form. There would be at least one full-court passing drill. And guards would almost always do step-slides with assistant coach Steve Robinson, working on the footwork that would enable them to become a better defensive team.

Before the NCAA Tournament, however, the step-slides suddenly ceased. Not because of a lack of practice time, but because Robinson—who works with the guards individually in practice while Joe Holladay works with the post players — wanted to challenge his players. Just before the first practice of the postseason, he took the guards aside.

"We're not going to do the step-slides anymore," he announced. "If you want to win a championship, you have to already know that it's important. If you don't want to win, you won't get better defensively. You won't stop your man. You won't contain the dribble. But if you want to win and you know it's important, you'll do it."

"At that point, everybody understood we had to get better defensively," Marcus Ginyard said. "We pulled together. Everybody was talking out there. Everybody was more aware of what was going on."

When Williams met the media on the day before the Gonzaga game, he admiringly said about the Bulldogs, "On the defensive end, every time you see the ball move, all five guys move." It was one of the highest compliments he would give another team, because it indicated a firm grasp of what he often calls "the big picture." For Williams, defense is more than just locking up in an individual battle against the man with the basketball. It's knowing what to do even when your man doesn't have the ball and understanding when to help a teammate.

Without much warning, and certainly without much fanfare, Williams's own team was about to become a very clear example of five guys moving.

CAROLINA AND GONZAGA WERE about as close to being sister programs as two schools on the opposite sides of the nation could be. That was largely because of the mutual admiration society made up of the two head coaches, as Williams and Mark Few had become friends during the summer recruiting circuit. On the night before they battled for the right to play in the final eight, the head coaches and their wives ate together at a Memphis restaurant.

The Tar Heel players were well acquainted with the Bulldogs. One of the pivotal games in the early careers of the current seniors was a Thanksgiving-week loss in 2006 to Gonzaga, when the underrated Zags toppled the second-ranked Tar Heels. That defeat remained fresh for the seniors, who understood the type of quality opponent they were facing in the round of 16.

"Before the Gonzaga game was one of my most nervous times," Frasor said. "I knew they were pretty good. They were well-coached. They had a lot of players."

That included three key members from the team that had bounced the Tar Heels before: Josh Heytvelt, Matt Bouldin, and Jeremy Pargo. That trio gave the Bulldogs as good an inside-outside combination as any team left in the

field, and Gonzaga became a popular upset pick among some members of the media.

But they would trail for 39 of the game's 40 minutes in one of Carolina's most complete dissections of a good team all season. The Tar Heels did it with defense, forcing the pesky Bouldin into 3-of-10 shooting and limiting Pargo to just two assists and three turnovers. They did it with offense, with four players in double figures and 52.9% shooting for the game. And they did it with coaching.

The Tar Heels held a double-digit lead for the final eight minutes of the first half and stretched the advantage to 17 points with 3:53 remaining on a three-pointer by Wayne Ellington. Gonzaga whittled the deficit to just 11 points by halftime, a manageable deficit considering the second-half LSU explosion in the previous round.

As the UNC coaches met before entering the locker room to discuss strategy with the players, the staff agreed: "The first five minutes of the second half are going to be key."

Williams nodded his head.

"They are," he said. "But I can't tell the team that. If they don't go well, I don't want the players to panic."

He needn't have worried. Six quick second-half points forced Few to call a time-out. Three minutes later, after Ellington converted a 4-on-1 fast break to push the lead to 21, Gonzaga had to burn another time-out.

The Bulldogs battled back. A steal and a layup by Pargo once again cut Carolina's lead to 11 points, at 68–57. Disgusted by turnovers and questionable shot selection, Williams again stepped out of character and called a time-out. He was concerned he might be watching an LSU repeat.

"This game is about North Carolina against Gonzaga," he told his team in the huddle. "It's not how many points you can make or what you can do individually. We have to make more intelligent decisions."

"He called that time-out to get us back into focus," Danny Green said. "It helped. We were turning the ball over and not getting the stops we needed. It was a smart time-out."

Coming out of the time-out, Williams called a set play designed to allow Ellington to set a screen and then come free off another screen. But Ty Lawson went the wrong way off the inbounds, which put Frasor into Ellington's spot.

Tyler Zeller played in the last 13 games. (Photo by Jim Hawkins)

opposite: Carolina avenged a 2006 loss to Gonzaga. (Photo by Jim Hawkins)

left: Deon Thompson nearly attended Gonzaga. (Photo by Jim Hawkins)

right: Bobby Frasor hit consecutive threes against Gonzaga. (Photo by Jim Hawkins)

Frasor set the screen, then Frasor received a screen and was suddenly open. He took the pass from Lawson and nailed a key three-pointer.

"Gonzaga was making a run at us and we called a time-out," Frasor said. "I got a great pass, stepped into it, and hit the shot."

Thirty seconds later, he did it again, this time in transition. Ellington had grabbed an errant Bulldog three-pointer and pushed the ball up the court. Frasor floated to the left wing, where Ellington found him for the second straight three-pointer. The lead would eventually balloon to 28 points, and Gonzaga would never be closer than 17 over the game's final 12 minutes.

The walk-ons earned a valuable two minutes of end-game playing time, giving the players in the regular rotation a chance to ponder the dismantling they had just inflicted on a solid team.

"We came out and we just buried them from the beginning," Frasor said. "That's when it really shocked me and I thought, 'Hey, we're playing pretty well right now. We can hang with anyone in this tournament.' . . . We were playing better than anybody in that field."

Scouting Gonzaga

Carolina lost to Gonzaga in the 2006 Preseason NIT, so when the teams each won their first two NCAA Tournament games, the top-seeded Tar Heels were on a collision course for redemption against the number-four-seed Bulldogs in a Sweet 16 showdown in Memphis.

Assistant coach C.B. McGrath prepared the scouting report for Roy Williams. McGrath watched the Zags play six times on tape—two NCAA games, the West Coast Conference final versus St. Mary's, a regular-season game against San Francisco (which is coached by Williams's protégé Rex Walters), their most recent loss to Memphis, and the previous UNC game.

McGrath wrote an extensive dossier for Williams, some of which would be shared with the players. The scouting report included general notes, tendencies, strengths and weaknesses for starters and key reserves, a breakdown of offensive and defensive sets, and even plays for out-of-bounds and jump-ball scenarios.

It ended with an executive summary entitled "What We Need to Do."

"This Gonzaga team was a lot like the one we played in New York," said McGrath. "They recruit skilled players who are good shooters and know how to play. And they play hard."

Three of Gonzaga's top four scorers—forward Josh Heytvelt, guard Matt Bouldin, and point guard Jeremy Pargo—combined for 49 points in the previous meeting. Heytvelt was credited with holding Tyler Hansbrough to nine points and afterward said he was surprised that the Carolina All-America shied away from contact.

McGrath's general notes stated: "Gonzaga is a very talented team with all the components to be great. . . . They beat us the last time and attacked us . . . . They will not be scared. . . . Their defensive field-goal percentage is 37.2. . . . They are a great shooting team. . . . They share the ball and are very unselfish . . . . They are the most explosive offensive team we've faced this year." Every scouting report lists three keys to the game. For Gonzaga, McGrath wrote:

1. Guard the ball—five guys alert to screen on the ball and be active.
2. Get the ball in the lane by dribble or pass.
3. Sprint back, pick up man, and get to shooters.

"The screen on the point of the ball is very difficult to cover," said Williams.

C.B. McGrath reviewing assignments with Danny Green. (Photo by Jim Hawkins)

"You have to decide who is the threat. Is it the dribbler or is it the slip guy? With Gonzaga, C.B. said, 'Coach, there's no question it's Heytvelt, it's [Micah] Downs, it's those guys slipping to the goal.'"

The Tar Heels typically are told to fight over screens, but Williams instructed the players to "squeeze" Gonzaga's screens. The player guarding the ball would sprint under the screener as quickly as possible. That risked giving up an occasional three, but it would allow the big men to prevent the screener from getting easy baskets.

"Ball screens are one of the hardest things to guard," said Bobby Frasor. "We were going to dare them to shoot so they couldn't get layups. And they didn't get one basket off of a slipped ball screen. They came out and were shooting really well from three and that kept them in the game. But it started going more and more to our advantage, and that's what separated us."

"C.B. did a marvelous job," said assistant coach Joe Holladay. "The only danger is the person could stop behind the screen and shoot, but they only made two baskets doing that. They were expecting us to step out and hedge and they'd set a game plan that way."

McGrath noted Heytvelt liked to get out in transition and run straight to the goal. Defending that is difficult because Gonzaga likes their other players to stop at the three-point line and shoot on the break. Hansbrough, Deon Thompson, and Ed Davis had to hustle back and deny the pass inside. At the same time, the perimeter defenders had to pick up shooters at the three-point line.

The scheme worked. Carolina had a 19–8 edge in fast-break points, and although the Zags hit six three-pointers in the first half, they made only 1 of

10 in the second. Bouldin, their best overall player, was 3 of 10 from the floor and 0 of 5 from three-point range, and he had no assists.

"Wayne Ellington, Bobby Frasor, and Danny Green did a good job defending Bouldin, and all four of our big guys defended well," said McGrath. "We didn't give up a slip-screen basket the entire game; we got back on defense and out on their shooters."

The Tar Heels shot the highest percentage all year against Gonzaga and took care of the ball too well to lose. Carolina shot 52.9%, committed only nine turnovers, and scored 98 points, also a season high against the Zags.

"When Wayne, Ty, and Danny shoot the ball like they did [8 for 16 from three-point range] we are pretty much unbeatable," said McGrath.

"My two biggest concerns were their big guys slipping to the basket and Tyler not getting so worked up about the last time we played them," said Williams. "Both of those turned out well for us."

Hansbrough had nine points by the half (equaling his output for the game in New York) and finished with 24 and 10 rebounds. Ellington and Lawson each scored 19, and Lawson and Green handed out nine and seven assists, respectively.

Carolina led by 11 at the half and by 21 with 15 minutes to play. The Zags eventually cut it to 11, but Frasor hit back-to-back three-pointers and the game was over.

"Two years ago, they got us real good," said Ellington. "We wanted to come out early and attack them. We all wanted to come out and fight. We knew they got us bad and we wanted to redeem ourselves."

For Gonzaga, it was a disappointing way to end another outstanding season. For the Tar Heels, it was on to the Elite Eight and the Oklahoma Sooners.

Ed Davis and the Tar Heels held the Zags to under 50% shooting in both halves. (Photo by Joe Murphy, Getty Images)

CHAPTER FIFTEEN

Five Guys Moving

"Be led by
your dreams,
not pushed
by your
problems."

Thought for the Day,
March 28, 2009

After Wayne Ellington, Ty Lawson, and Danny Green had returned to school in the summer of 2008, they were on the floor for one of the numerous Smith Center summer pickup games. As usual, the game was a mix of current and former Tar Heels, with plenty of NBA talent on the floor. Teams are thrown together on the spur of the moment, their compositions based more on time of arrival at the gym than on the need for a team to be fully stocked with each of the five positions.

In one game, a perimeter-heavy team of Lawson, Green, Ellington, Bobby Frasor, and Tyler Hansbrough was matched against a squad that featured 2005 Final Four Most Outstanding Player Sean May at the power-forward position. That left Green guarding May and forced the other four players to keep constant awareness of when help was needed, with a healthy dose of rotating to help cover the opponent's guards when May was being double-teamed.

"It's funny that that happened during the summer," Ellington said. "Because we had to do the same kind of thing against Oklahoma in the regional final. We're playing to go to the Final Four, and we're doing the exact same thing we did in the summer. That's where experience helped, because we had already done it one time."

This time, the post presence demanding attention was 2009 National Player of the Year Blake Griffin. The Sooner sophomore had been the 2008–09 season's most consistently dominating force, averaging 22.7 points and 14.4 rebounds per game. He suffered a concussion late in the regular season against Texas; in his absence, the Sooners lost four of six games, which left them out of the hunt for a number-one seed.

Steve Robinson had the scouting duties against Oklahoma, and he'd watched the Sooners' 84–71 victory over Syracuse from a courtside seat, filling a legal pad with notes and observations. Because of the late tip-off time for the game against Gonzaga, the Tar Heels had barely 36 hours to prepare for the regional final. Despite the slim preparation time, those 36 hours would contain one of the most important strategic decisions of the season.

Throughout his coaching career, Dean Smith preferred to spend his squad's practice time honing their skills rather than preparing for the variations in an upcoming opponent's attack. "We didn't give our players extensive information about an opponent, because we wanted them to concentrate on our own execution and the way we played. We had a stubborn streak," Smith wrote in his memoir, *A Coach's Life*. Williams had inherited that belief. "I don't want to take what you want to give me," he repeated often after returning to Chapel Hill in 2003. "I want to take what I want."

Observers sometimes confused that philosophy with inflexibility. In reality, the 2008–09 season saw many adjustments by the Tar Heels. They placed more importance on ball screens to take advantage of Ty Lawson's skills, and they changed the way they inbounded the ball because of early-season struggles in that department. Tweaks in the Gonzaga game plan slowed one of the nation's most efficient offenses. With the right to play in the Final Four at stake, the staff would make one more key modification.

The original scouting report Robinson filed with Williams indicated a need to double-team immediately on Griffin's first move after catching the ball in the post. The head coach believed waiting for the big man to make a move might be too late. After watching a second Oklahoma game tape, he approached Robinson. Carolina's normal principle was for the player creating the double-team to drop halfway into the post, wait for a move, and then drop into the double-team. Williams and Robinson decided to order the double-teaming player to drop onto Griffin immediately, with no waiting for a move.

It was more complicated than just a blanket "double-team Griffin" order. The coaching staff had to decide where the double-team should come from and how they wanted to camouflage the openings created by playing three defenders against the remaining four Oklahoma players. Sooner sharpshooter Tony Crocker had blistered Syracuse for 28 points, including six three-pointers, in the round of 16, so placing increased emphasis on Griffin was not without its risks.

"Once we decided to double Blake every time he caught the basketball, we

Danny Green was sensational against the Sooners. (Photo by Joe Murphy, Getty Images)

had to decide what to do with the rest of them," Joe Holladay said. "We decided to come off of the guy who had passed it into the post. Then everybody else would rotate around and on the rotation, the man who was the first trapper would take the guy on the opposite side after the ball came out. It was a complete rotation."

It was also a rotation that required a great deal of movement and communication. Another possibility the staff considered was for the Tar Heel who was defending the least effective shooter to drop into the double-team on Griffin. But that required all five players to know the stats and threat level of the five Sooners on the floor at all times. With the chosen method, the rotation would be thorough, but it would also be the same on every possession.

There was just one practice between the win over Gonzaga and the regional final. At that practice, the staff instructed their team on the defensive strategy against the Sooners.

"A huge part of our practice that day was working on the double-teamer jamming down," Williams said. "We wanted to jam down and double with the defensive player who had played the passer. When that happened, we had to rotate over. When that guy did double down, if there was a pass back out, we had to get the proper rotation to get him back into position."

After 15 minutes of drilling the approach against Griffin, Williams looked at Robinson. "We're going to be fine," he said.

The game's other variable was the one-on-one matchup between Griffin and Tyler Hansbrough. Throughout his career, the Carolina senior had consistently dismissed any suggestion of individual battles, often claiming that he watched so little college basketball that he didn't assign any special significance to a specific opponent. As a junior, he publicly pretended not to know the identity of NC State freshman J.J. Hickson. As a senior, he had played down the matchup with Notre Dame's Luke Harangody while privately being goaded by teammates about "Hansgody."

Now, with Griffin, his public statements claiming not to know much about the Sooner star weren't exactly true. He hadn't sat down to watch endless game film or analyzed his own strengths and weaknesses in comparison to Griffin. But he definitely knew all about the attention Griffin had received—to the point that several team members were pleased to see Oklahoma as the region's second seed because they felt playing against Griffin would bring out the best in Hansbrough.

But a true individual battle never developed. As it turned out, the most one-on-one time they spent together was when the referees gathered the game captains at midcourt 13 minutes before tip-off. Like two boxers getting prefight instructions, they stood in the center jump circle without looking at each other, even looking off into the distance while bumping fists.

"If it had been my freshman year, I probably would've tried to go at him every possession one-on-one," Hansbrough said. "But I've matured, and I realized there's something more important here. That's winning a national championship."

Five different Tar Heels—a quintet that did not include Hansbrough—scored during a 13–2 run in the game's first six minutes. Both Green and Ellington made jumpers during that stretch, and Ellington noticed a sense of foreboding from the Sooners.

"Teams emphasize taking the jumper away from us," he said. "When we do knock down a jumper, they have that feeling like, 'Hopefully neither one of those guys gets started.' When we knock down one or two in a row, they start feeling, 'Oh gosh, this could get ugly.' And when we're clicking from the inside and the outside, I feel like teams think we can't be stopped."

Oklahoma's own unstoppable force, Griffin, attempted just one field goal in the first 12 minutes of the game. Part of that drought was due to Carolina's fast-moving double-team strategy. But Griffin's struggles were also due in part to the work the Tar Heel post players did before he ever caught the ball.

The Carolina coaches call it "working early," and it was exactly what Deon Thompson had done with such success against Clemson's Trevor Booker earlier in the season. Letting Griffin—or Booker—catch the ball on the low block almost guaranteed two points. That meant the post quartet of Hansbrough, Thompson, Ed Davis, and Tyler Zeller—the four players who would spend time guarding Griffin—would have to give their best defensive effort before Griffin's teammates passed him the ball.

Thompson, especially, had evolved into a solid post defender who understood how to use the combination of his muscle and his brain to thwart his opponent's best moves. The coaches knew how essential his role was, and he landed the bulk of the individual assignment on Griffin.

"Deon has good feet," Robinson said. "You can't let that guy get to his spot and turn around and post up with you behind him. You have to work early, so maybe you push him out one or two steps further. Now he's not in the comfort zone where he wants to be. And Deon is capable of defending that way."

Eventually, the swarming Tar Heel defense seemed to affect Griffin.

"He just stood there in the first half," Holladay said. "When he caught the ball, he was waiting on the double-team to come because he knew he was going to be doubled."

But just limiting Griffin wouldn't be enough to earn a Final Four berth. While the posts were banging with the National Player of the Year, the wings and guards had to make sure they knew where all of Oklahoma's perimeter shooting threats were located. Williams knew he could easily design a defense to limit one player; limiting one player while simultaneously cutting off the other offensive options was more challenging.

Late in the first half, the quintet of Lawson, Green, Davis, Ellington, and Thompson forced Oklahoma to melt 34 seconds off the shot clock before Crocker missed a desperation three-pointer. On the next Sooner possession, the same five forced a shot-clock violation.

Incredibly, Oklahoma would not make a shot outside the paint until five minutes remained in the game. The Sooners definitely missed some shots they would ordinarily make. But some of the credit for their poor shooting had to go to the Tar Heel defense, which might have played its most complete game of the season.

The stingy defense was supplemented by an opportunistic offense that was

run to perfection by Lawson. In addition to scoring (a team-high 19 points) and passing (a team-high five assists), the junior also showed some vocal leadership. When Oklahoma made a rare push, Green tried a high-risk long bounce pass between two defenders. Surprisingly, it was Lawson who reprimanded him. "Take care of the ball!" Lawson barked on the court.

"I felt like I needed to become one of the leaders," Lawson said. "Tyler and Bobby are leaders, but by example. Danny is a leader, but he doesn't talk much on the court. I needed to be the one to get in people's faces when they made a mistake. As I started doing that, I felt more comfortable with the role."

Oklahoma never crept closer than nine points in the second half, and the

left: Ty Lawson won regional MVP honors. (Photo by J. D. Lyon Jr.)

right: Tar Heels celebrated with Chancellor Holden Thorp. (Photo by J. D. Lyon Jr.)

opposite: The last two National Players of the Year. (Photo by Joe Murphy, Getty Images)

lead eventually stretched to 21 points. In fact, it was when the lead reached 21, at 61–40, that Hansbrough experienced his only slip of the game. Finally, the urge to take on Griffin grew too strong to ignore. And so Hansbrough—who had memorably dunked on UNC Asheville's 7-foot-7 Kenny George as a junior—tried an ill-conceived dunk attempt over Griffin that almost resembled a hook shot more than a dunk. Physics made it almost impossible to dunk a ball from the distance Hansbrough attempted.

In the next timeout, Williams went around the huddle pointing out his team's most recent errors. Then he gave his senior an incredulous look.

"And Tyler!" Williams said. "Tyler's trying to freaking dunk it from 35 feet out!"

With a 21-point lead and just six minutes left, it was okay for Hansbrough to stifle a smile. In just a few minutes, he'd be clutching his second straight regional championship trophy.

An Academic Championship

As difficult as it is to win a national championship in basketball, the University of North Carolina achieved an even rarer feat in 2009.

The season brought not only an NCAA championship on the court for the Tar Heels but also a national title in the classroom. After the release of the NCAA Tournament bracket in March, *Inside Higher Ed* magazine analyzed the field and advanced those teams with the better academic performance in each matchup. Carolina emerged as the overall winner based on its Academic Progress Rate (APR).

The APR is the NCAA's formula for measuring academic progress, giving credit to programs whose student-athletes stay enrolled and in good standing academically. The Carolina men's basketball team has been honored by the NCAA in each of the last two years for posting an APR in the top 10 percent nationally.

A lot of coaches at a lot of basketball programs claim to emphasize their players' academic success as much as wins on the court, but few do it as well as Roy Williams at North Carolina.

"It was very rewarding, very satisfying to win the national championship of the APR," Williams said. "To me, that side of our program is extremely important. I love it when they show a list of coaches in *USA Today* and beside Roy Williams's name it had the highest APR. I love it when they show those brackets and the last team standing was North Carolina."

In NCAA statistics released in January 2009, Carolina's four-year APR of 995 was the highest of any school in the six major athletic conferences in the nation.

All seven seniors on the 2009 national-championship roster walked with their class during graduation ceremonies at Kenan Stadium on May 10. In Williams's six seasons since he returned to UNC in 2003, every Tar Heel senior player has earned his degree or is on track to do so.

Several players who left school early for the NBA have been regulars at summer school in Chapel Hill to continue work on their degrees, including Sean May and Marvin Williams (who left after his freshman season in 2005 and is now a junior academically).

President Barack Obama praised the team for their academic achievements during UNC's visit to the White House on May 11.

"I know Coach Williams instills the importance of academics into all of

President Obama saluted the Tar Heels for winning the academic bracket. (Photo by Jeffrey A. Camarati)

these guys," the president said. "Which is why they didn't just plow through the tournament, they also had the highest graduation rate. What they understood is that being a champion doesn't stop when you step off the court."

In all of his 21 seasons as a head coach, Williams has trusted one man to guide the academic progress of every player he's ever coached: Wayne Walden, who deserves some of the credit for the team's excellence in the classroom.

"It's funny, because I say it in every [recruit's] home: 'Our academic guy is the best,'" Williams said. "I'd rather lose every assistant coach together than lose Wayne Walden."

The players concurred.

"Another thing that we can say about this program and about this team is that we can continue to stay focused knowing that we have schoolwork on top of all the things that we have to worry about," said senior Marcus Ginyard. "Obviously, we have Wayne Walden, and without him, I think it would be impossible for me. He does a great job keeping us in line and—just like everything else in this program—keeps everything running smoothly."

Roy Williams with Wayne Walden, his top academic adviser for 21 years. (Photo by Jeffrey A. Camarati)

It's especially challenging to stay up-to-date academically while traveling so much throughout the season, particularly in March.

"It's tough because you're on the road and you may have an assignment when you get back, or a test, and you might not want to think about school, to be honest with you," Bobby Frasor said. "You know it's the NCAA Tournament, but you have to get your work done despite it all."

To gauge the challenge of keeping 17 players on top of their schoolwork during the NCAA Tournament, consider that, during the run to the 2009 national title, Carolina players missed nine of 14 class days while traveling. Study halls in hotel meeting rooms and late-night sessions in Chapel Hill between games were essential.

"The month of March obviously is difficult," Walden said. "Fortunately, we've got faculty that are willing to work with them and have always been very good about allowing them to turn in things later or by e-mail. Especially with freshmen, where that's a brand new experience for them; they just have no idea what to expect, and they're the main ones in study hall on the road."

When players return to Chapel Hill in the fall of 2009, they'll have to do it without Walden. The Topeka, Kansas, native left Carolina in the summer of 2009 to get married and move to Texas to live with his new bride, Leslie. Williams is left to face one of his worst nightmares: replacing Walden.

"He's been tough on the kids," said a teary-eyed Williams as he announced Walden's impending departure at the team's end-of-the-season award ceremony in April. "Some of them have appreciated him more than others. Every one will appreciate him at the end. I just want you to know that I have been lucky to be at Kansas, I've been lucky to be at the University of North Carolina, I've been lucky to have these kinds of players you see in front of you now—but I've been *really* lucky to have the academic adviser that I've had for 21 years. Wayne, thank you."

CHAPTER SIXTEEN

Business Trip

In many ways, the Peabody Hotel in Memphis had been the perfect team hotel. Its huge lobby had ample room for the band, cheerleaders, and hordes of fans for team send-offs and after-game gatherings. It was within easy walking distance of a wide selection of good restaurants. And it had a wide variety of sizable meeting rooms for team functions.

The Hilton Garden Inn in Detroit had none of those amenities. And Roy Williams thought it was perfect, which was exactly why he picked it.

The NCAA gave participating teams two options for hotels. They could stay in a ritzier property, but they would be housed at least 20 minutes outside downtown Detroit. Or they could sacrifice some creature comforts and opt for downtown hotels. Most coaches chose the more comfortable property, but Williams—even though the Tar Heels traditionally stay in high-quality hotels throughout the season—did not.

For most of the six-night stay, live bands performed loudly or badly—often both—for most of the afternoon and evening hours. The Garden Inn's accommodations were so basic that Ty Lawson and Wayne Ellington joked about their room's tiny size. Overhearing the conversation, Williams said, "Hey guys, you want to come see my 'suite?'" The head coach's room was barely bigger than the bathrooms at some of the hotels where the team had stayed.

But Williams knew the trip was not about finding a five-star hotel. The trip was about winning a national championship, and he believed a downtown hotel did the best job of facilitating that goal. The Tar Heels bused to and from practices and games in Detroit, where they were driven as usual by the squad's quasi-official bus driver, "Super" Dave Harder. But it actually might have been faster to walk the two blocks from the hotel to the arena.

"I chose to stay there because it was the closest [to Ford Field]," Williams said. "I wanted our guys to be involved in the atmosphere of the Final Four and realize they were at the Final Four, but I didn't want any delays in getting

"Be led by your dreams, not pushed by your problems."
Thought for the Day, April 1 and 2, 2009

"This was the first time in my four years at Carolina that Coach Williams kept repeating the same thought for the day on the practice plan. It means: don't worry about things that could go wrong; don't think of all the negatives. Think positively about what we have to do to win a national championship."
—Bobby Frasor

to practice. I didn't want any delays in getting to the building. I wanted to be there."

ON THE FRIDAY before the national semifinals, Connecticut head coach Jim Calhoun uttered a statement that sent a shiver through the Tar Heel fan base.

"They space the court as well [as] if not better than any team I've seen recently," Calhoun said of Villanova, a team Calhoun's Huskies had faced during the regular season.

That was exactly the type of offensive attack that had periodically caused problems for the Tar Heels. Spreading the floor, locating the mismatch, and beating a defender off the dribble had resulted in high-scoring games for guards from Wake Forest and Florida State.

"We knew they were going to spread the floor on us and they were going to try and drive on us and make plays," Ellington said. "That's the type of team they are."

After all the defensive machinations against Oklahoma, this would be much simpler. It would be basketball at its most basic: one man dribbling, another man trying to stop him.

"If you don't control the basketball when the other team spreads the floor on you, they're going to dribble-penetrate on you all night," Williams said.

"You've got to get back in to help or they'll pitch out, or if they get all the way to the basket your big guy has to help and they get easy baskets. It was a big emphasis for us to control the basketball. You are responsible for your man. You know your teammates will be there, but don't depend on it. You guard your man."

The men they would be guarding were very familiar to the Tar Heel backcourt. Lawson had extensive AAU basketball experience playing both with and against several Wildcats, and he exchanged text messages with a handful of Villanova players during Final Four week.

Ellington, a Philadelphia native who spurned the Wildcats during the recruiting process, had played for 'Nova head coach Jay Wright with the U.S. Pan American team in the summer of 2007. That meant he had already been exposed to Wright's frenetic sideline style; Ellington cracked a grin during the national semifinal when he heard Wright rip one of his players at high volume during the game.

"He was definitely saying some things that sounded familiar," Ellington said.

The UNC guards knew they faced a formidable challenge against the guard-heavy Wildcats. Quietly, however, the Tar Heels felt they had a substantial edge in the paint, where Villanova couldn't match their size, athleticism, or depth.

"Our advantage was our size," Deon Thompson said. "Coach has won a lot of games and knows how to win games. He emphasized getting the ball inside either by dribble or by passing the ball.... And they were so worried about our inside guys, they forgot we had all our talented shooters on the perimeter."

That the Tar Heels were worried about the opponent and not the environment was a significant change from the 2008 Final Four. In that season, a sense of relief accompanied Carolina to San Antonio. They'd spent the season trying to exorcise the disappointment of a 2007 regional final meltdown against Georgetown. Reaching the 2008 Final Four had felt like a major achievement.

This year, however, reaching the 2009 Final Four simply seemed like a natural progression. Everything was routine, from the pre-event banquet with all four teams to the open practice on Friday in the cavernous Ford Field.

"The previous year helped us a lot," Green said. "We weren't just happy to be there. We weren't shocked or excited by all the people and the lights and how big the dome was. Last year when we went to the Final Four, we lost focus. But this year we came in confident and ready to play. We were a more mature team."

The lasting number from the 2008 trip had been the 40–12 lead built by Kansas midway through the first half. This year, it was almost an exact reversal. With seven minutes left in the first half, the Tar Heels had a 40–23 lead.

Just like the previous year, however, that huge bulge wouldn't hold. Villanova narrowed their deficit to 49–40 at halftime and crept within 50–45 two minutes into the second half. The comeback was fueled by Scottie Reynolds, one of Lawson's childhood friends, who dropped in a couple of jumpers. It was not a matter of Carolina frittering away the lead. It was simply an awakening for a team that had played a starstruck first half.

At the next time-out, Williams assessed the situation with his team.

"Guys, it's not easy to win a national championship," he said. "These guys are good, or they wouldn't be here. They are not going to roll over for you. Don't expect them to miss shots for you. Don't play defense wishing that they would miss. Play defense demanding that they miss because of how you play them."

His team did begin to play demanding defense. They also tossed in an unexpected wrinkle, as foul trouble forced the Tar Heels into a zone for eight

Ty Lawson driving on childhood friend Scottie Reynolds. (Photo by Bob Donnan)

second-half possessions. The mix of man-to-man and zone limited the Wildcats to just 26.3% shooting in the second half. For the game, Villanova would shoot just 18.5% from the three-point line.

The UNC offense didn't play its sharpest game of the postseason, but it was helped by an unexpected source: Bobby Frasor's rebounding. The Tar Heel senior had been giddy all week about the prospect of playing in his first career Final Four. He made the trip in 2008 but couldn't play in the game because of a knee injury, and he spent most of Final Four weekend in 2009 with a video camera pressed to his eye, recording every pep rally and celebration for posterity.

His enthusiasm carried over into the game, where he didn't score a point but pulled down a career-high five offensive rebounds. Three of those offensive boards came during a key stretch in the second half, as the Tar Heels increased the lead from five points to an eventual 18-point bulge. It was the perfect snapshot of what differentiates a merely talented team from a championship team. On a championship team, players not only understand what their role is; they also understand what their role isn't. Scoring was a bonus from Frasor, but hustle was a requirement. Fortunately for the Tar Heels, he was perfectly suited to provide it.

"To be in the Final Four was a dream of mine growing up as a kid," Frasor said. "I ran out onto that court with a smile on my face. I was so happy to be there. Then, to be a part of it and get five offensive rebounds and be a key contributor in the win made the feeling even better. They weren't boxing me out. I had a free run to the basket every time. I had a good sense of where the rebound was going to go. To extend a possession, it makes the other team feel like, 'Now we've got to play defense even longer against these guys.'"

"His effort guarding the ball, sharing the basketball, coming up with big rebounds and big plays was exactly what we needed," Steve Robinson said. "He provided that little spark for us by sheer effort. He never hesitated one time."

Frasor, who also won the team's defensive award for the game, was on the floor at the end as Carolina wrapped up an 83–69 victory. Immediately after the game, one of the Tar Heel assistants proclaimed it the best game he had ever seen from a player who didn't score a point. As he frequently does, Joe

Holladay made a circuit around the locker room, saying something individually to each player.

"You broke their hearts," he told Frasor. "Every time they stopped us, you
gave us another chance."

In most cases, Williams asks his team to enjoy wins until midnight before
turning their focus to the next opponent. This time, the win didn't linger that
long. Before the locker room was opened to the media for postgame interviews, the head coach gave his team a frank assessment of their chances in the
national championship game against hometown favorite Michigan State.

"Guys, people say we can't beat somebody two times," he said. "You can
beat them 20 times in a row if you're better. We beat them up here by 35,
and we can beat them again. Those people in the stands aren't going to come
down and play. I like this scenario, because people say we can't do it, but we
can do it. You're better than they are. Between now and Monday night, get
that in your mind. You're better than they are, and Monday night we get to
go play."

Frasor's Storybook Ending

January 26, 2009, began like most Mondays in Bobby Frasor's final semester as a Tar Heel. Sleep in a little, get to his eleven o'clock corporate strategies class, and check out the *Daily Tar Heel*, Carolina's student newspaper. Except that morning's paper contained a letter to the editor with this boldface headline: "In light of poor season, Frasor should play less." It essentially implied that Frasor is a nice guy and quite likeable, but that he was neither shooting nor defending well enough to warrant the playing time Roy Williams was giving him.

Well, good morning to you—and thanks for that poison-pen dose of school spirit.

Frasor, for whom the term "savvy senior leader" was seemingly invented, read the paper at the Student Union. He was sure that many of the other 28,000 or so UNC students read it, too, and was somewhat embarrassed by its contents. He was about 20 games into the season, struggling to regain the form he had prior to reconstructive knee surgery, and here came a campus debate about his minutes and value to the team.

The versatile guard from Blue Island, Illinois, was backing up both Ty Lawson and Wayne Ellington roughly a year after blowing out his left knee. Just getting back on the floor had been no simple task. He had yet to play like the gritty freshman who started all 31 games and led the Tar Heels to a win at top-ranked Duke to spoil J.J. Redick's senior night in 2006.

"When you first get out on the court, you're a little hesitant to do a move or push off your leg that you had surgery on," said Frasor. "It did take me longer than expected. Coach Williams said no matter how hard you work, it's probably not realistic to get back to where you were before you hurt your knee."

Frasor injured his ACL against Nevada on December 27, 2007, and missed that season's final 26 games. He made it back for the 2008–09 opener against Penn, but he subsequently hit just 11 of his first 48 three-point attempts.

"Offensively, I kind of lost that killer instinct," said Frasor. "It hurt me sometimes thinking about that at night or staying up and just wondering what happened to my game. But then I kind of accepted my new role . . . just being a great defender, hustling, getting loose balls, making some shots if the ball comes my way."

The comfort level appeared first at Duke, two weeks after the notorious letter to the editor. Frasor matched his career high with three first-half three-pointers, almost equaling the combined output from Tyler Hansbrough, Lawson, and Ellington. He helped keep the Tar Heels within striking distance of the inspired Blue Devils. In the second half, Carolina hammered its hosts, outscoring them by 22 points and winning 101–87.

"I finally said, 'Hey, just go out there and have fun,'" said Frasor. "That's what my grandfather always told me. I thought about writing a letter to the *DTH*, but I would have made it comical, saying, 'Hey, what do you have to say now?' But to have a moment like that when you are a big part of a win and the team needed you, it was kind of saying, 'Yeah, I can still play.'"

Williams never doubted Frasor's value, which was essential to a team with championship dreams.

"Bobby's a great leader, our best defender, especially with Marcus [Ginyard] out of the lineup. . . . [He] takes care of the ball and had the courage to knock down a big shot when we needed one," said Williams. "I've never had a player battle as much adversity throughout his career as Bobby has with the injuries, but his attitude and commitment to helping us win a championship never wavered."

Frasor started three games in the ACC and NCAA Tournaments when Lawson was dealing with an injury of his own. He had 13 assists in those games and showed again he was capable of leading a team in the postseason. But it was his "do anything to win" approach that made him a favorite of both Carolina fans and his coaches.

Against Radford in the first round of the NCAA Tournament, he pushed the ball up court for seven assists in a lopsided win; in the Sweet 16, he made a pair of second-half threes that iced Gonzaga; and in the Final Four, he gave two defensive-player-

Bobby Frasor made three long-distance shots at Duke. (Photo by Robert Crawford)

of-the-game performances that helped the Tar Heels cut down the nets. He even grabbed a career-high five offensive rebounds in the national semifinal against Villanova.

After the 83–69 win over the Wildcats, assistant coach Steve Robinson said Frasor played one of the best games he'd ever seen by a player who didn't score a single point.

Two nights later, Frasor celebrated after playing 23 error-free minutes against Michigan State. He scored one final basket as a Tar Heel, then he watched his dad, Bob, who coached him in high school, revel in his son's success.

"My dad was a kid in a candy shop," said Frasor. "He was so happy. Tears were running down his face. You never really see your dad in tears. For a basketball game to bring that emotion out of him, for me to play well, to win a national championship, cut down a piece of the net, turn over and look at my family and hold that net up for them—it's something I'm never going to forget."

So, Mr. *DTH* Letter Writer, what do you have to say now?

CHAPTER SEVENTEEN

Waiting

What do you do when you reach the point in your life that you've always dreamed about, the moment that will—for better or worse—shape the perception people have of you for years and decades to come?

You wait.

By the time the Tar Heels left Ford Field on Saturday night, it was after midnight. That left approximately 45 hours until the tip-off of the national championship game. For the players, the first 10 of those hours were spent sleeping. For the coaches, there was game tape to watch, scouting reports to finalize, and game plans to formulate. As soon as the Tar Heels finished dispatching Villanova, Michigan State held a team meeting at their hotel to go over UNC personnel and tendencies. Carolina didn't have that luxury, although everyone remembered the first meeting of the year between the two teams.

Most of the players had a lazy Sunday morning. The coaches were already going over their Michigan State game plans. C.B. McGrath had the Spartan scouting assignment, just as he had in the first meeting in December. MSU wasn't exactly the same team; this time they would have Goran Suton, who sat out the December matchup with an injury. But the rest of the personnel was the same, and McGrath relayed his observations on the April version of the Spartans to the coaching staff.

"Their toughness concerns me," he said. "All their tough wins, like Louisville, UConn, and Kansas, were close games until Michigan State refused to be denied. They execute their offense, they play great defensively, and they get the rebounds they needed to get. I hope our guys don't overlook them or think it will happen easily because we beat them so badly the first time.

"They were a more confident team than the one we played in December," he continued. "Suton gave them confidence, something that made them believe, 'Hey, we're a different team.' And they were a different team. You don't beat Louisville and UConn and not be a better, more confident team."

After breakfast, the first scheduled events for the players were early-after-

"Be led by your dreams, not pushed by your problems."
Thought for the Day, April 3, 2009

"It tells us exactly what Coach wanted us to focus on. He could have said so many things to us, but that one quote covered it all. It says to focus on the passion we have for the game, the excitement we have about playing in the Final Four and our goal of winning the whole thing."
—Marcus Ginyard

Danny Green was injured against Villanova. (Photo by Jeffrey A. Camarati)

opposite:
top: Ty Lawson's remarks drew a laugh from Coach Williams at Sunday's press conference. (Photo by Jim Hawkins)

center: Killing time during press conferences. (Photo by Jim Hawkins)

bottom: Even Roy has to wait. (Photo by Jim Hawkins)

noon media obligations back at Ford Field. At those press conferences, while the Spartan players entertained the eager local press, the Tar Heels looked, quite frankly, like a team that had been playing basketball until midnight the night before.

After the press conferences, the team went through a light practice, made even lighter by the injury to Danny Green. He had strained an oblique muscle in the previous night's victory, an injury that hadn't concerned him at the time. But it grew sorer as the night progressed, even when he iced it on Saturday night. By Sunday, Green couldn't run, jump, or even laugh.

"If we played the game today, could you play?" Roy Williams asked him.

"I don't think so," Green said.

"Wow—not even for the national championship?"

"Coach, I really can't move much at all."

Green became Chris Hirth's new project, with a constant mix of ice and heat to try and enable the senior to play. In public, the injury was never mentioned. Most fans never knew how close Green came to missing the title game.

Two key points were reviewed at the afternoon practice: the importance of rebounding and the importance of getting back on defense. Carolina had the well-earned reputation as a transition team, but Michigan State also liked to run, usually by taking advantage of a team lazily retreating on defense. Because the Spartans weren't overwhelming offensively, getting easy baskets in transition was a key part of their offense.

An evening meeting back at the hotel showed the typical personality of the 2009 Tar Heels. With just over 24 hours until they played for a national championship, most of the players were more concerned with a phenomenon they called the "Soggy Booty Boys." No one knew exactly where it had started, but it had become a highlight of most team functions.

The goal was simple: at a team meeting or meal,

one or two players would try to soak the chair of an unsuspecting team-mate—sometimes even a coach. If that player or coach sat down in the wet chair, he would immediately be greeted with raucous shouts of "Soggy Booty Boy!"

"It just shows how immature we are," Bobby Frasor said. "We're college students. It's something we had fun with all year."

All year, including the night before the national title game.

"Ty got me the night before the game," Mike Copeland said. "I wasn't even thinking about it. He got me good, because he had soaked the whole chair. I sat down, and I didn't feel it at first. Then I realized the whole thing was soaked."

Eric Hoots was also a victim in Detroit. To a passerby hearing the shrieks of glee from inside the team meeting room, you might have thought Williams had asked the players to visualize their excitement if they won a national championship. Instead, they were just delighting in yet another member of the Soggy Booty Boys.

A very long 24 hours remained until game time.

ROY WILLIAMS'S GAME-DAY TRADITION, like most of his traditions, hadn't changed much during his coaching career. As usual, he woke up early and went walking—it used to be a jog—with a few friends. And, as usual, he hoped one of them would fall down.

That particular superstition was created in 1991, when a member of his coaching staff slipped and fell while jogging through the streets of Louisville before an NCAA Tournament game against Pittsburgh. "That's paying the price," Williams said. "That's a really good sign." The Jayhawks played well against the Panthers, and a superstition was born. From that point forward, any time a member of Williams's group fell on game day, it was considered a good omen.

The morning of the championship game dawned gray with a light snow. Williams rounded up his group of walkers and, well, he couldn't help but smile as he recounted the story.

"Everybody's cold, and we're bundled up with the toboggans, the gloves, the towels, and everything," Williams said. "[Ticket manager] Clint Gwaltney ran head first into a stop sign. It knocked his hat off, he stumbled a little bit, and I was so concerned that I was right there shouting, 'That's as good as falling! It's the same thing!' His head could've been bleeding, I didn't care. Coach Holladay and I were cheering so hard, we thought it was the greatest thing."

Williams had amended his tradition in Memphis, where he supplemented

the group walk with a 30-minute walk by himself. He used it to clear his head and make sure he was focused on the most important facets of the day. He ate a quick meal, then accompanied the team to a light shootaround at Ford Field, which by now was starting to feel like a second home. The streets were already filling with Michigan State fans. On one side of Brush Street, the road that connected the hotel with Ford Field, a group of fans would shout, "Go Green!" They would be answered almost immediately by a group responding, "Go White!" The players barely noticed.

At shootaround, Danny Green gauged his mobility. He definitely couldn't dunk, but he could fire jump shots. He couldn't pass the ball across his body, which eliminated the cross-court and no-look passes he loved. But he could shoot, and he could pass, and he could slide his feet enough to capably defend.

"Okay," Green said. "I can do this."

Back at the hotel, Williams dismissed his players with these words: "This is what we practiced for. This is why we ran in the fall. This is why we hurt so badly after the Kansas game last year. This is what you've put yourself in position to do. Let's enjoy it. Don't try to win the game at 3:00 in the afternoon. Get your rest, we'll eat a pregame meal, we'll go to the game, we'll talk about it, and then we'll go play."

Game time. (Photo by Bob Donnan)

As the players soon learned, Williams made it sound easier than it actually was. Most of the players and coaches had family members in Detroit to watch the game, and most hung out with their families at least a little bit on Monday afternoon.

Steve Robinson eventually banished most of his family to an adjoining room. That left him free to ponder the upcoming evening, and he decided he wanted to do one important thing differently in 2009 than he had done in

2005. "This time, I wanted to get some confetti," he said of the brightly colored streamers that would be released from the ceiling when the final seconds elapsed. In 2005 he'd been so caught up in the moment he failed to recover any souvenirs. This time, he wanted to be prepared.

Down the hall, Tyler Hansbrough was submitting to a secret vice: VH1.

"Most people don't know it, but I'm a huge VH1 fan," he said of the music television channel. "Bobby makes fun of me all the time. I watched a lot of VH1 that afternoon."

It was one of the rare times, however, that even Frasor couldn't crack a joke. He was sitting on the bed in his room flipping through channels repeatedly, never stopping for more than a few seconds on any one show. Asked later, he couldn't even remember any of the shows he had seen. It was pure nervous energy, the desire to occupy himself with anything, even something as mundane as scanning through channels. No one wanted to watch ESPN, which was filled with pregame title talk.

Even the team's most unlikely candidate for nerves found he was affected. Ty Lawson traditionally was a prime candidate for a pregame nap, even in the minutes before tip-off. There had been times during his freshman season when he had to be reminded to tie his shoes before entering the game. But now, so close to a championship, nerves hit him hard.

As usual, the team ate their pregame meal four hours before tip. Lawson turned to Copeland and said, "I can't eat. I don't know why, but I can't eat."

"You're excited," Copeland said.

"Yeah, man," Lawson said, pushing his plate away. "I just can't eat right now."

At Ford Field, with the roar of 72,922 fans audible even inside the locker room deep within the hallways of the arena, Williams reviewed the game plan with his team before he sent them onto the court for the last time.

"We've got to get back on defense," he told them. "We've got to build a wall to stop their penetration. And I want you to box out, and I don't want you to let us down on one single possession with that. It's not okay to say, 'My bad, Coach, I didn't box him out.' That crap is gone. Don't look over at the bench and say, 'My fault.' I expect you to play well. I expect you to run back. I expect you to box out."

Then he ended with a message that still gave goose bumps to some team members a month later.

"Somebody's going to win the game tonight," he said. "Somebody is going to win a national championship. Why not let it be us?"

Keeping the Faith

Each year, Carolina Basketball players list what their favorite *SportsCenter* highlight would be. Before the 2008–09 season, Deon Thompson, UNC's 6-foot-8 power forward, wrote: "Game-winning shot in the Final Four."

Officially, Danny Green's three-pointer gave the Tar Heels a 5–3 lead over Michigan State—a lead that they would not relinquish. But Thompson had scored the game's first basket and added seven more first-half points as Carolina raced to a record 55–34 lead.

"Deon's buckets were maybe the most important for us," said Roy Williams. "They were emphasizing covering Tyler [Hansbrough] so much that Deon was always just one-on-one, and there was nobody coming toward him and he made shots."

Thompson's play against the Spartans fulfilled the notion most observers had all year about the Tar Heels: when all five starters were hitting shots and making plays, Carolina was unbeatable.

The Torrance, California, native's play was stellar that night in Detroit, but his play all season was admittedly marked by inconsistency. He was spectacular early, steady throughout, rarely flashy, yet memorable in several key games. How many players would love to say their four most impressive efforts were against Kentucky, Notre Dame, Duke on the road, and in the national championship game?

Thompson opened the season—with Hansbrough in street clothes because of injury—with a career-high 17 points against Penn, topping that performance three days later against Kentucky with 20 points and nine rebounds.

"It was a time for me to see that I can play on this level and actually be successful and help a team win," said Thompson. "It showed me I could be a big part of wins."

Thompson scored in double figures in each of the first 12 games, shooting 59 percent from the floor. Beginning in January, however, his longest stretch of double-figure-scoring games was three, and he shot 47 percent from the floor in the last 12 games.

Some questioned whether he could flourish playing with another low-post threat like Hansbrough, but Thompson was sensational against Notre Dame in Maui, notching 19 points, a career-best 13 rebounds, two steals, and a thunderous dunk on a night when Hansbrough scored 34. So much for the notion that Thompson could only shine without the 2008 Player of the Year on the floor.

"It was maintaining that intensity over the course of a long season," said Williams. "Deon has gotten so much better physically, but not letting little things bother him mentally, that's been a more difficult struggle for him."

Of course, it's not easy being the so-called fifth option on a team with Hansbrough, Ty Lawson, Wayne Ellington, and Green. It's like being a fifth Beatle: you may be a great musician, but it's hard to get much attention when John, Paul, George, and Ringo are out front.

But the affable Thompson never thought of that as a problem.

"We are all one collective group. Coach always preaches to enjoy each other's successes. If the team is winning, we are all winning. You can't let not getting the ball or seeing your name in the clippings the next day affect you."

Senior leader Marcus Ginyard talked frequently to both Thompson and Bobby Frasor about always being ready to make an impact even though "you're not that first, second, or third scoring option."

At Duke, Thompson scuttled the Blue Devils' defensive plan to lay off him and double-team Hansbrough as he scored 10 points in the first seven minutes, helping the Tar Heels build a 25–16 lead.

However, Thompson struggled in the NCAA Tournament at the same time that 6-foot-10 freshman Ed Davis was playing his best basketball, leading some to wonder if Williams would make a move in the starting lineup. But Thompson stayed put and rewarded Williams with a decisive first half in the national championship game.

"If I'm scoring like that," he said, "and guys are getting stops—we come down the floor and Tyler scores, then Ty drives past you, then Wayne makes a three, then Danny makes a three—it's almost like, 'Pick your poison.' It showed in the first few minutes that we were a machine on a mission.

Deon Thompson said Roy Williams is a second father to him. (Photo by Streeter Lecka, Getty Images)

Deon Thompson scored in double figures 22 times.
(Photo by Brian Fleming)

"Coach never lost faith in me, and I knew God would eventually come through," added Thompson. "God is always on time, and I am pretty sure he showed up at the right time on one of the biggest days for me."

"I told him to be more aggressive and post deep," said Lawson. "I wanted him to get in the paint and get easy shots. That is what he did, and he played amazing in the first half."

Thompson credited Williams for helping him mature as a person and a player.

"I used to get down on myself because I wanted to be the best I could be right then, right now. I learned to be patient and remind myself that I was new to the game. I learned it is just a game and you have to have fun."

One memorable image from the celebration is that of Thompson and Williams draped arm in arm as the coach shed a tear while watching CBS's "One Shining Moment."

"I love honesty, and that is the best thing Coach is going to give you every time you talk to him," said Thompson. "He is a second father to me. I put my arm around him, and he felt comfortable enough to let a tear fall and enjoy that one shining moment. To know that he gives everything he has when he coaches our team and develops young men into men. In a moment like that, you just feel everything you worked hard for is accomplished. All your goals are met. It is a complete satisfaction for him, and definitely for me."

CHAPTER EIGHTEEN

Champions

The Tar Heels were greeted with a chorus of boos as they took the court. To celebrate the 30th anniversary of the classic 1979 NCAA championship game between Michigan State and Indiana State, Spartan alum Magic Johnson and ISU alum Larry Bird were presenting the official game ball. After a ceremony at midcourt, each legend shook hands with Roy Williams and Tom Izzo.

Williams told Johnson, "Don't worry, I know who you're rooting for."

But then, when Bird approached the bench, he leaned in close to Williams and said, "Beat their butt for me. I want to talk some junk to Magic."

That scored even more points for Bird with Tyler Hansbrough, who already considered Bird one of his favorite players of all time.

"That makes me like him even more," Hansbrough said when he was told later about Bird's comments.

The game's opening tip was bizarre, as an immediate tie-up ball meant Hansbrough had to rejump against Michigan State's 6-foot-2 Travis Walton. It brought to mind an image of Carolina sending out 5-foot-11 Tommy Kearns to jump center against Wilt Chamberlain in the 1957 title game. The taller Hansbrough won the tip, and on the game's first possession, Deon Thompson took the ball aggressively to the basket, spinning to the hoop against freshman Delvon Roe — a former Tar Heel recruit — and dropping it through. When the coaches reviewed the game film, they would marvel at Thompson's move. "That's just a flat-out tough shot," C.B. McGrath said. On the bench, everyone knew what it meant. When Thompson's offense started hot, it was usually a harbinger of a good game to come.

Suton answered with a three-pointer, but Danny Green answered with a three-pointer of his own. Then, on the next Spartan possession, the Carolina coaches saw a much more encouraging sign. Forced into a half-court offense because every Tar Heel sprinted back hard on defense, the Spartans tried to run a play designed to create a lob to Raymar Morgan. But that exact play had been on the UNC scouting report, and Green knew the high, arcing pass was

"Be led by your dreams, not pushed by your problems."

Thought for the Day, April 5, 2009

Deon Thompson had nine of UNC's 55 first-half points. (Photo by Jim Hawkins)

opposite: Wayne Ellington had 17 first-half points. (Photo by Bob Donnan)

coming. With McGrath off the bench screaming, "Lob!," Green followed Morgan down the lane and eliminated the angle, forcing the first of 21 Michigan State turnovers.

Wayne Ellington sliced through the lane for a 7–3 lead, but on the bench, the coaches noticed what he did after the basket more than what he did to create the hoop. As soon as the ball dropped through the net, Ellington turned and dashed to the other end of the court, ready to play defense. That was the kind of awareness Williams had been preaching all season. Ellington's hustle cut off a potential fast-break chance for Walton and might have symbolized the story of the game. With all five Tar Heels sprinting back on defense—the only noticeable full-court breakdown was when Ed Davis was beaten for a layup early in the half—Michigan State's transition opportunities were slim.

Then, in the half-court offense, tenacious man-to-man meant that none of the Spartans' set plays resulted in easy baskets. The formula was simple: great hustle plus great help and support in the half-court equaled exceptional defense. Most MSU possessions ended with a turnover or a contested jump shot, the kind of attempt Williams liked even if it found the basket. If his team matched MSU's grit and the game turned into a battle to see which team's offensive personnel could create the best shots, the Tar Heels knew they had the advantage. Privately, the Tar Heel coaches felt they had good enough offense to win the game without great defense if the offense was clicking. They also felt they were good enough on defense to win without great offense if the defense was clicking. But pair great defense with great offense and there was little doubt about the outcome.

"We had so much confidence and energy," Ty Lawson said. "That was what we had worked so hard for in the off-season. We put in the late nights at the gym, running with Jonas [Sahratian] during the summer and lifting weights. All the blood, sweat, and tears came down to this moment and we wanted to win so badly."

It showed. Six different Tar Heels scored in the game's first five and a half minutes. When Hansbrough posted up on the left block and turned to his right shoulder to fire a textbook turnaround jumper that made it 17–7, the players thought they began to feel some doubt creeping into the Spartans. Carolina, after all, had throttled this same team by 35 points in this same venue just four months earlier. For all the talk about how it would be a differ-

left: One of Tyler Hansbrough's favorite shots as a Tar Heel. (Photo by Bob Donnan)

right: Ty Lawson had six assists in the title game. (Photo by John Biever, *Sports Illustrated*)

ent game, a big early deficit had to raise the question of whether the Tar Heels were simply that much better than Michigan State.

Lawson knew he could freelance defensively in the backcourt. After Davis dropped through a nearly impossible layup, contorting his body to take the ball from behind the backboard to the rim, Draymond Green threw a lazy in-bounds pass to Kalin Lucas. Lawson sprinted from six feet away while the ball was in the air to grab the steal—one of eight he would pilfer during the game—wrestling it away from Lucas. That play led to a 21–7 lead, and the Tar Heels had the Spartans up against the ropes, pounding away in an effort to land a haymaker.

"I put more emphasis on defense in the first half," Lawson said. "I wanted to stop Lucas because he was a catalyst for his team. If he played well, the rest of their team played well. I wanted to get in his face and get easy steals, make his life hard the whole game."

Even when Lawson left the game for the first time, with 13:38 left in the first half, the Tar Heel offense continued to click. With Larry Drew II running the point, Carolina continued to have one of its best screening games of the season. There had been times during the year when screens had been soft, with the screener not making contact with the defender. This time, everything was solid. Davis set a high screen for Ellington while inside, Bobby Frasor set a chest-shaking screen for Thompson. That pick freed the junior to run uncontested to the low block, where Drew found him with an easy bounce pass. Throughout the season, the coaching staff had admonished Thompson and Hansbrough to "post lower," meaning they wanted the big men to fight to receive the ball even closer to the basket and to get it where they wanted it, not where the defense wanted them to get it. The screens created that room inside, giving Thompson the ball exactly where he wanted it—exactly where the entire Carolina offense was designed to run—and it resulted in another hoop and a 24–8 lead.

The quintessential play of the game may have come with 10:30 left in the half. Thompson battled for a tough defensive rebound, once again limiting the Spartans to just one shot. He found Lawson for an outlet pass above the three-point line, and the Tar Heel point guard relayed the ball to Ellington, who was already on the wing in front of the Michigan State bench, 22 feet from the hoop. Ellington looked inside and found Hansbrough, who had already established post position. Hansbrough scored to provide a 31–11 lead. The whole sequence took less than eight seconds, and it was a perfect snippet of ideal Carolina Basketball.

"At one point, I said, 'They can't stop us,'" Steve Robinson remembered.

It certainly had to feel that way for Tom Izzo. Before the game, the Michigan State head coach had told his team in the locker room, "They're going to have some runs; that is who they are. We have to keep those runs to four to six points, not eight to 12. I don't want to use time-outs all the time early to stop runs."

But when Ellington came off a double screen and squared up in front of the Spartan bench before nailing another three-pointer, Izzo had no choice. With Carolina holding a 43–20 lead and 6:45 remaining in the half, Michigan State called its first time-out of the half.

"Coach Williams talked to me after the game and told me I better have made that shot," Ellington said with a smile. "When I saw that one go in, I was like, 'Yeah, I'm rolling right now.' It was one of the toughest shots I've taken, and when that one dropped for me, it felt great. It was kind of like a dagger because it was such a tough shot and I don't think many people expected it to go in."

Considering the circumstances, environment, and opponent, it was one of the most dominating halves ever played by a Tar Heel team. Every member of the rotation contributed on offense and defense, and at one point Williams had three freshmen—Drew II, Davis, and Tyler Zeller—on the court at the same time and the rookies held the lead, a sign that perhaps the season's numerous injuries had been beneficial in allowing the freshmen to be comfortable in a pressure-packed environment.

Williams never looks at the scoreboard during the first half, preferring to gauge his team on how he sees them play rather than what the score is. He saw it for the first time as he left the Ford Field court, taking a glance that was too quick for him to be certain of the margin. So his first question upon arriving in the coaches' locker room was, "What is the score?"

"We're up by 21," his staff told him.

Indeed, the margin was 55–34, the largest halftime lead in NCAA championship-game history.

"It was not a perfect half," Williams said. "But for the national championship game, it was the perfect half."

That was not the message he delivered to his team, of course.

As the players waited for the coaches to join them in the locker room, they knew exactly what the score was. They also knew exactly what that score meant: they were 20 minutes away from a national championship.

"We were talking about what we thought was going on back in Chapel Hill and at home," Thompson said. "We were talking about how we were going to celebrate. Honestly, we got a little distracted."

It was Williams's job to get them refocused. After consulting with his staff, the coaches joined the players. His halftime message included a reminder of the task faced by the 2008 team in coming back against Kansas, a comeback that was nearly successful.

"Guys, we were down 28 to Kansas last year, and we had a shot to make it a one-possession game," Williams said. "How did Michigan State get here? Because of their mental toughness and because of how they competed. I told you before the game that our want-to can't just match theirs, it has to be more than theirs. They're going to come back. They're going to make a run. Our want-to still has to exceed theirs."

top: Ty Lawson and
Roy Williams shared a
special embrace when
Lawson left the floor
for the final time as
a Tar Heel. (Photo by
Jeffrey A. Camarati)

bottom: The Carolina
bench erupted when
the final buzzer rang
in Detroit. (Photo
by Gregory Shamus,
Getty Images)

left: Senior tricaptain Danny Green raised the championship trophy with his teammates. (Photo by Jeffrey A. Camarati)

right: Roy Williams said this handshake and hug from Tyler Hansbrough was a moment he will cherish forever. (Photo by Andy Lyons, Getty Images)

The Spartans did get within 15 points with 9:32 remaining, but that was as close as they would get when the game was still in doubt. They finally carved the deficit under 15 points with five minutes left—and with a national title in the balance, even that felt tenuous—but four straight points from Lawson and a Frasor layup quickly pushed the lead back out to 19.

On the bench, the countdown was on.

That distraction did not extend to the head coach. Carolina had never won a national title without the starters on the floor. The previous championship

games were so close that the head coaches were never able to clear the bench. This time, with a 17-point advantage and less than two minutes remaining, Williams nudged McGrath. "Get those last five," he told his assistant.

With 1:03 remaining and an 87–70 lead, J.B. Tanner, Patrick Moody, Justin Watts, Marc Campbell, and Mike Copeland entered the game. The party was beginning on Franklin Street. But on the bench, the meaning of sending in his substitutes hadn't hit Williams.

"I knew what the score was and I knew I was putting the last five guys in the game, but it still hadn't dawned on me that we're winning the national championship," Williams said. "I know that sounds crazy. When Tyler came walking over to me with that big grin on his face, he hugged me and it almost knocked me down. I have never seen a look of joy on a kid's face like that in my entire life. At that moment, I realized what that game meant to me."

Sixty-three seconds later, the final buzzer sounded and streamers fired from the ceiling with loud pops. Robinson reached into his pocket, where he had kept a plastic bag all night for exactly this purpose. He scooped up some streamers, happy that he had planned ahead this time.

Across the court, Hansbrough sprinted over in front of the Tar Heel cheering section, where he exulted in front of his family and friends.

"In the middle of the year, when Tyler was still battling the injury, we were talking about whether it had been a good idea to come back," Frasor said. "He said, 'If we win a national championship, of course it was.' You could see how happy he was that night, jumping around by himself and pumping his fist with all the confetti falling. It was a great feeling to be part of it and a great sight to see."

When the team assembled on the podium to receive the national championship trophy and watch "One Shining Moment" together, Ellington was brought to tears. He had just been named the Most Outstanding Player of the Final Four.

"It was the best journey of my life . . . that I will ever have in my life," he said. "That's something nobody can ever take away from us. We worked so hard, and we've been through so much, and we did it. That hits me in my heart, and that's something I'm always going to get emotional about for the rest of my life."

The Tar Heels retreated to the locker room together and celebrated as a team. Following a last round of interviews, they were driven across town to accept another championship trophy at a downtown hotel. Only then were they allowed to return to their hotel, where fans and family members waited for them. After some jubilant hugs, the team met one last time as a group for a postgame meal in a bottom-floor hotel banquet room.

Only one final task was left to accomplish. A conniving player tried to soak Williams's chair with an ice cube, but the head coach was too savvy to fall for the trick. Jonas Sahratian was not as fortunate; he sat down on a completely soaked chair.

For the final time, the 2008–09 Tar Heels reveled as a team. With perplexed hotel staff waiting outside the doors, the players roared, "Soggy Booty Boy!"

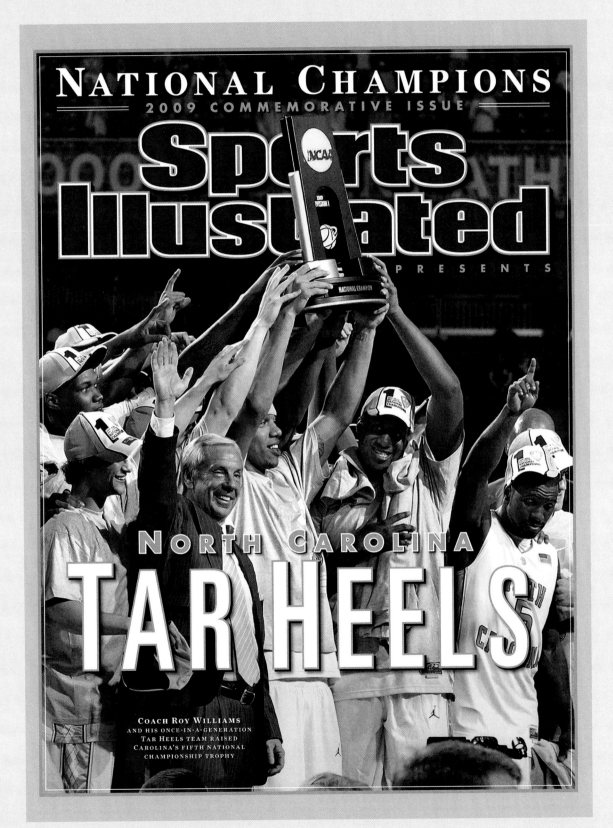

NATIONAL CHAMPIONS

2009 COMMEMORATIVE ISSUE

Sports Illustrated

PRESENTS

NORTH CAROLINA
TAR HEELS

COACH ROY WILLIAMS
AND HIS ONCE-IN-A-GENERATION
TAR HEELS TEAM RAISED
CAROLINA'S FIFTH NATIONAL
CHAMPIONSHIP TROPHY

Photo by John Biever, *Sports Illustrated*

The fans on Franklin Street in Chapel Hill partied like it was . . . 2005! (Photo by Andrew Dye, *Daily Tar Heel*)

Taking His Shot

It was just minutes before the tip-off of the national championship game against Michigan State, and Wayne Ellington was worried.

In his warm-up routine before every Carolina game, he liked to move around the court and make shots from certain spots on the floor, always ending his ritual superstitiously with a made three-pointer before leaving the court.

Except on this night—of all nights—he couldn't buy a basket. After the rest of his teammates had returned to the bench, and as Magic Johnson and Larry Bird walked to midcourt for a pregame ceremony honoring the 30th anniversary of their meeting in the 1979 NCAA championship game, Ellington shot again and again, unable to drain one from behind the three-point arc.

"It was funny that that happened to me, because up until then, I was making my last one almost every time," Ellington said. After the tip-off, Ellington made his first shot, a two-pointer less than two minutes into the game.

"When I made my first one," he said, "I was like, 'Phew.' I didn't realize anyone else realized that but me."

He went on to pour in 17 first-half points, hitting 7 of 9 shots and all three of his three-point tries as the Tar Heels built a commanding 55–34 lead at the break. Ellington earned Final Four Most Outstanding Player honors after the game, echoing the trajectory of his season: an inauspicious beginning followed by a dazzling ending.

After testing the NBA waters and returning to school in the summer, Ellington started the year slowly, struggling with his shot and not scoring 20 points until the Miami game, the 18th contest of the season.

Against the Hurricanes in Chapel Hill that night, he broke out of his slump in a big way, scoring 23 points and hitting seven consecutive three-pointers in the second half. Four days later against Clemson, Ellington scored 25 points, and the slump was history.

"After the Virginia game [January 15], I met with Coach Williams, and he said, 'You know, you just have to have one of those games where you hit about three or four straight and you're going to be fine from there,'" said Ellington. "The next game it happened for me. I think from there I got my confidence back, I got my rhythm back."

As he struggled with his shot, Ellington focused on expanding the breadth of his game.

"I went through a little time where it was tough for me and I had to do other things, I had to contribute," he said. "So, I stepped up in other areas of my game."

Against Maryland in early February, Ellington again hit seven three-pointers and grabbed a career-best nine rebounds. Two weeks later at Miami, he posted his first career double-double with 15 points and 10 boards, and he dished out five assists against just one turnover.

"I've always pushed him to be a more complete player — rebound the ball, take the ball to the basket, get fouled, defend people," Williams said. "I think that he really bought into it when the shot wasn't going in, trying to do those other things."

On the season, Ellington posted a career high in assists and rebounds and significantly improved his assist-turnover ratio. Impressively, he led Carolina in rebounding against Atlantic Coast Conference opponents. Ellington's coaches and teammates voted him UNC's most improved player, an honor he shared with freshman Ed Davis.

"He became a guy that wasn't one-dimensional," Steve Robinson said. "All of a sudden he explodes against Clemson and explodes against Miami, and I think from that point on, the light bulb was on and the confidence was back. He just picked a great time period to start playing his best basketball."

Ellington continued to improve into the postseason, scoring in double figures in 25 of the last 26 games. He averaged 19.5 points and 6.5 rebounds in the Final Four, hitting a record 8 of 10 three-point attempts in the two wins. Overall in the NCAA Tournament, he hit 17 of 32 three-point tries (53.1%).

Despite his long early-season slump, Ellington persevered and prevailed on the college game's biggest stage. Ultimately, he gave part of the credit to his father, Wayne Ellington Sr., for some words of advice a decade earlier.

"It was after my sixth-grade year," the younger Ellington recalled. "We were 52–0, and we were in the championship game and we're down one, I think, with like nine seconds left. I got the ball, faked one way, took one dribble, and I pulled up and I made it to win the game. And we ended up 53–0. So, I was really excited and really happy [and] my teammates were

Wayne Ellington joined UNC's James Worthy, Donald Williams, and Sean May as Final Four Most Outstanding Players. (Photo by Andy Lyons, Getty Images)

Wayne Ellington is UNC's 18th-leading career scorer. (Photo by Bob Donnan)

jumping on me. And after the game, my dad was excited, but he didn't show too much emotion. I got in the car . . . and he said, 'Great players take those kinds of shots, great players have the confidence and the courage to take those kinds of shots, whether they make them or miss them.'"

Ellington took his father's words to heart and, to the benefit of Carolina Basketball's 2009 championship hopes, put them into action in the most important game of his college career.

The Storybook

On the first day of the second session of summer school in 2005, Bobby Frasor and Tyler Hansbrough moved in together. They were not quite strangers, as they'd encountered each other on the high school all-star circuit, but they weren't friends yet, either. On one side of the room, Hansbrough set out three laundry bags for dirty clothes—one for darks, one for whites, and one for towels. On the other side, Frasor kicked a couple of shirts aside to clear space for what would eventually become his dirty-laundry pile.

It was a perfect case of opposites attracting—thanks to the rooming assignments of the UNC coaches. Frasor talked constantly; Hansbrough rarely spoke at all. Frasor was a city boy from a suburb of Chicago; Hansbrough relished his small-town home of Poplar Bluff, Missouri. And somehow, Roy Williams needed this odd-couple duo to combine with Marcus Ginyard, Danny Green, and Mike Copeland to form a nucleus freshman class that would prevent Tar Heel basketball from suffering the fall everyone predicted in the wake of the NBA mass exodus after the 2005 national title.

"I remember walking up to Tyler on that day and trying to say, 'What's up?'" Frasor said. "He goes, 'What's up, big man?' That's what he called everybody. He didn't know how to call you by your name. His vocabulary wasn't that extensive.

"On day one, I thought he was a little strange. By day two, he was already lying, saying he had been the quarterback of his high school football team. He tried to bring up a picture on the Internet to show that it's him, and it was just some guy in a helmet. At that point I knew he was a character, just like I was."

The whole class was full of characters. What made them unique was that they were always a group, always together. From their freshman year forward, if you saw one of them, at least one or two of the others would be right behind him. Down the hall, Green and Ginyard were adjusting to life as roommates.

Green was a sports fanatic whose life soundtrack was a bouncing basketball. Ginyard preferred not to watch sports.

"The first couple of months getting used to Marcus, there were some things I thought I could put up with and some things I thought I couldn't," Green said. "He has to blast his music and he has to get up early, and he'll walk around the room without too much clothing on. But Marcus has always been my guy, and we know everything about each other."

Almost instantly, Frasor became the perfect foil for Hansbrough. Other teammates weren't certain how to take the big man, but Frasor always knew exactly how to twist the proverbial knife, sometimes without Hansbrough even realizing it.

"I joke with him all the time that he would have left school after his freshman or sophomore year if I wasn't at Carolina," Frasor said. "I was kind of the mediator between everybody else and him. If somebody wanted to ask him a question, they'd probably come to me."

"They were both here for one reason," Joe Holladay said. "They both came to be a part of something big. Bobby's helped Tyler expand because Tyler has

to fight back. Bobby will just sit there and rip you, and if you don't fight back, it'll never stop. They've been great for each other."

Hansbrough's off-court growth was substantial, but it was tinged with the unique characteristics that made him great on the court. By his senior year, he was comfortable playing the board game Catchphrase with strangers. But even when paired with a partner he didn't know, he still would not allow any mistakes. Once, when his partner slipped and cost them the game, Hansbrough bellowed, "Don't cheat yourself!" Everyone else's eyes widened—and then the group dissolved into laughter.

The seniors formed the foundation of what might be one of the last teams of its kind: a group that spurned repeated NBA opportunities to make one final push for a national championship. By the time they were seniors, they'd been in virtually every big game and spent endless time with each other off the court. Surprises simply didn't happen.

"The things that happen off the court directly influence what happens on the court," said Jerod Haase, who played for Williams at Kansas. "That's what chemistry is. It's how you get along, it's the experiences you have when you're

Senior Marcus Ginyard.
(Photo by Jeffrey A. Camarati)

away from the court, it's the experiences you have at the late-night snacks on the road. All of those things help a team become a little bit more tight-knit."

They began as talented but raw freshmen. At a Chapel Hill coaching clinic in the fall of 2005, several coaches with UNC ties were skeptical as Williams outlined his plans for his freshmen—Hansbrough in particular. This young player was going to have that type of impact in the Atlantic Coast Conference? It seemed improbable at best, yet Williams was essentially placing the immediate fate of the program in Hansbrough's hands.

Williams's instincts were quickly proven right. In the team's first road ACC game, the Tar Heels pulled out a 64–61 victory at Virginia Tech. Hansbrough made two clutch free throws with 9.3 seconds left to seal the victory.

"That's when I really thought, 'I can play in this league and really do something big,'" Hansbrough said. "Everybody talked about how tough ACC play is. To have a big game really helped my confidence, and it carried on throughout my whole career."

"When you come to Carolina, you have somewhere in the back of your mind the knowledge that you're going to be held to a higher standard," Marcus Ginyard said. "Coming in as freshmen [after a national championship] was a great situation for our class. Being able to gradually feel that confidence, to be able to handle that pressure and still perform, was important. This class did a great job of showing leadership and showing the confidence in the players that we can do what people expect us to do and what we expect of ourselves."

As the players fulfilled some of those goals, the bond between Roy Williams and his first Tar Heel "nucleus class" grew. By the time they were seniors, he knew they understood how to respond to any situation, whether on or off the court. Williams displayed outward confidence in Memphis and throughout the rest of the NCAA Tournament because he knew he had a great team. But it was also because he trusted his players to make the right plays.

"Coach trusts our players because they're great kids,"

Haase said. "They've done what he's asked them to do on a continual basis. It started with Bobby, Tyler, Marcus, and Danny showing up at 7:00 A.M. at the weight room continuously right when they got here. That trust has been building for four years. The seniors just haven't done a whole lot wrong. They've built that trust time after time."

It's almost impossible to believe that two years ago, it looked like the legacy of the class might be a dream unfulfilled. In a disappointing end to the 2006–07 season, the Tar Heels frittered away a 15-point lead against Georgetown in the regional final, unable to get the offense running through Hansbrough, win the game, and get to the Final Four. The previous season, they'd lost a surprise second-round game to upstart George Mason.

As they did throughout their four years, they came back. They eventually set numerous school records, winning at least 30 games for three straight years for the first time in school history. The wins alone were enough to endear them to the Carolina fan base, of course. But they always seemed to connect on a deeper level because they seemed to fully understand what it meant to go to the University of North Carolina. They were regulars at the Sutton's Drug Store lunch counter. They participated in the community; Ginyard was honored at the athletic department's end-of-year banquet as one of six student-athletes with outstanding commitment to community service and outreach programs.

Bobby Frasor claimed "World's Greatest Athlete" status after defeating his fellow seniors in an off-season "Olympics." (Photo by Emma Patti, *Daily Tar Heel*)

"Coach does a great job recruiting great people," Green said. "Not just great players, but great people. The kids that come in here are good kids with great attitudes. It would be different if he recruited guys from different places with bad attitudes. The chemistry wouldn't be as good as it is. We're like brothers. We are a big family."

They depart as a family of winners, with a national championship banner hanging in the Smith Center rafters. It is one of the rare times in the current era of college basketball that a team grew up together and left with the ultimate prize. Too often, modern fans are denied the privilege of watching players learn and develop. On and off the court, this group went through a complete metamorphosis, from freshmen too inexperienced to sustain the great success of 2005 to seniors who were predicted—no, expected—to become legendary.

Remarkably, there was a segment of the basketball world that believed this class had to win a national title to validate its greatness. Over four years, these players had won virtually every important game, but some believed until they won that last game of the season, their legacy would always have an asterisk.

On the march to Detroit, the players largely downplayed that line of thinking. But they were aware of it.

"There were so many questions leading up to the tournament about whether I would be a great college player if we didn't win a national championship," Hansbrough said. "I was kind of mad people were asking me that. There's a lot of great college players who haven't won a national championship, and I felt like they were writing me off. They wanted a reason to write me off for not being a good player. When we won, that lifted all that pressure from all those critics. To finally prove ourselves and be in that position was something special."

"This is the storybook ending," Frasor said. "We started off as freshmen, and no one expected anything from us. We got better and closer each year. And then to win it all in our fourth and final year, to be able to sit up there and watch 'One Shining Moment' with our teammates holding the national championship trophy — it's a fairy-tale ending."

And what of that Hansbrough-Frasor relationship that began four years ago in a Granville Towers dorm room? The quiet big man wants you to know he's more well-rounded now. He's added some rap songs to his iPod, his TV tastes have expanded, and he eagerly looks forward to every opportunity to fly.

Well, maybe not that last one.

Asked about Frasor, Hansbrough grinned.

"First of all, he doesn't go to sleep until 3:30 in the morning," he said. "He always gets mad at me for going to sleep at midnight. He always makes fun of me by saying, 'I'm going to drink a protein shake and go to sleep,' because that's what he thinks I do. Also, he's so messy. He reuses his dirty clothes, and he used to not take showers for a couple days. That's why he got his nickname: Dirty Bobby. Yeah, there are some weird tendencies that I have, but he definitely has his, too."

With that, Hansbrough smiled in satisfaction. He had several National Player of the Year awards and a national championship. This might have been the first time, however, that he received something even more rare among this group of extroverts—the last word.

Finishing on Top

History will show that Carolina won the 2009 NCAA title on April 6 in Detroit, but in many ways the heavy lifting for securing the championship trophy took place 994 miles due south of Ford Field on a late January night in Tallahassee, Florida.

The Tar Heels beat Florida State, 80–77, on a breathtaking last-second three-pointer by Ty Lawson. That was exciting, but what made the night so meaningful was Tyler Hansbrough's boyishly joyous reaction to Lawson's heroics. The All-America drew three early fouls and was held to eight points, snapping a streak of 55 consecutive double-figure performances, which was within shouting distance of the UNC record. When Lawson hit the shot, Hansbrough was the first to reach him, lifting him in the air with a wild look in his eyes and a smile from ear to ear.

That moment again confirmed that Hansbrough was about only one thing: winning. And he didn't care who got the job done.

"He was the first guy to grab me and try to pick me up," said Lawson. "All he wanted was to win. He has done everything else. He's been player of the year, his name is going to be in the rafters, he has the scoring record. All he wanted to do was win a national championship."

There had never been jealousy among his teammates—remarkable considering Hansbrough commanded attention from day one of his freshman year with his fierce play, productivity, and trophy case full of accolades and awards. But that night in Tallahassee demonstrated he was ready for others to step forward and share in the spotlight—mainly Lawson, Wayne Ellington, and Danny Green.

"To see how happy Tyler was that we won the game and that's all that mattered, that was huge for those other guys to say, 'Wow, it's amazing. The player of the year came back and he doesn't care that he's not getting all these touches, all these points, all this attention,'" said Bobby Frasor, Hansbrough's roommate for four years and his best friend. "We're winning basketball games, and that's what he came back for."

The Poplar Bluff, Missouri, native won every major national player-of-the-year honor as a junior and then became the first in almost 20 years to win those awards and return to college. He dealt with adversity all season, from the stress reaction in his shin to the media backlash that was termed

"Tyler fatigue" and the pressure of trying to finish his storied career with a championship.

"I was a better player this year, but also I was a more mature player," said Hansbrough. "I understood there are some really good players on this team. So I thought, . . . 'Let's just get the ball to Ty and see what happens.' I didn't really learn until my senior year that sometimes to win, you're going to have to do the little things, and whenever your team needs you to score, that's when you can do that."

The Florida State game was one of only three times this year that Hansbrough was held under 10 points. (He scored eight at Miami and against Oklahoma in the NCAA South Regional final.) In games at FSU and Miami, he made key defensive stops in the final minute that helped the Tar Heels win; and against the Sooners, he avoided getting into a game of one-upmanship with 2009 player of the year Blake Griffin. With the Final Four on the line, he had three assists and took only four shots, concentrating on defense and rebounding and allowing Lawson, Green, and Deon Thompson to do the damage offensively.

"There were times when I felt more comfortable with Ty having the ball, or

Wayne," he said. "But I understood my part, and that was really important for this team, and it was contagious."

"Tyler could have come out and gotten 30 a game, and he very easily could have been player of the year again," said Frasor. "He realized that we had to step up, all of us, and get a better all-around type of game for us to be national champions. For him to have done that means a lot to all of us. That was a big-time part of us being national champions, no question."

Even with a slightly changed role, Hansbrough spent his senior season rewriting the college basketball record books. He became the ACC's all-time scoring leader, first breaking Phil Ford's Tar Heel mark against Evansville and then the ACC record against Radford in the NCAA Tournament. He broke Sam Perkins's UNC record for rebounds, Johnny Dawkins's ACC record for double-figure scoring games, J.J. Redick's ACC mark for 20-point contests, and Ford's UNC record for field goals. In his second-to-last home game, he broke the NCAA record for free throws made, an enduring legacy for a 6-foot-9 forward who got to the foul line more than 1,200 times in his career.

"When you play with a guy like Tyler Hansbrough, who's broken every record at Carolina and broke NCAA records, and his jersey's retired, it's something to be proud of," said Ellington. "It's going to be an honor to sit down and tell my kids I played with a guy who was that caliber of player. He didn't go about it in any type of selfish way. He went about it within our team concept, and that's huge."

College kids by nature are not easily impressed, especially basketball players, who almost to a man have been told how great they are since they first began to dribble a ball. But listening to the Tar Heels talk about Hansbrough shows you the level of respect they have for their teammate and friend.

Frasor: "It's hard saying it now because it sounds super-cheesy, but the reality of it is when I have kids and grandkids, I'm going to take them into the Smith Center, point to the rafters at the No. 50 jersey, and say, 'I lived with this guy. I was really close friends with him. We won a national championship together.' It's pretty cool. It's the only way I can describe it."

Green: "I was able to watch him day in and day out for four years. He works so hard and has been so consistent for us and it paid off in the end. To be a part of that and to tell a story like that to your grandkids is always good. It was an honor for me to be a part of that and to be a teammate of his."

Marcus Ginyard: "The first thing when I tell people about my college days will be, 'Oh yeah, I played at Carolina with Tyler Hansbrough when he was

Carolina fans came out in large numbers at each NCAA Tournament open practice. (Photo by Robert Crawford)

beating up everybody.' There's no question that you're sitting at the barber shop 20 years from now, and . . . you're talking for an hour, and 30 minutes is going to be about the big guy and all the stuff he did here, the way that he was able to help lead this team by example."

The "Big Fella," as Roy Williams calls Hansbrough, would probably cringe reading those words of praise, but he does appreciate the history he has authored here. He knows that his place in college basketball is secure as one of the best—if not *the* best—to ever play at North Carolina.

"It's an indescribable feeling," he said. "I've watched Carolina since I was little. I remember when they first called me and I was in my gym, I was shocked they were even recruiting me. When I came here, I thought I was going to be good but never imagined I'd be where I am. For me to be considered up there with Michael Jordan and Phil Ford and Antawn Jamison and that front row, that's amazing."

Hansbrough reached heights few college basketball players ever have: four-time first-team All-America, four-time first-team All-ACC, 124 wins, three ACC regular-season titles, two ACC Tournament titles, three NCAA number-one seeds, two Final Fours, a national championship, National Player of the Year and ACC Athlete of the Year awards; and yet two of his proudest days came a month after his final game, when on consecutive days in May, he graduated with his class at Kenan Stadium and visited the White House to meet with President Barack Obama.

"It was important for me to get that degree and walk in the stadium with the guys I came to Carolina with four years ago," he said proudly. "And going to see the president meant we had reached the dream we came to Carolina for. It's going to be a great feeling when they hang that national championship banner and seeing everybody come back for that, all my teammates, and hanging out after we've played. That will be fun."

CHAPTER TWENTY

The Program

After 10:00 P.M. on April 14, 2003, Roy Williams sat in front of a bank of microphones and said some very prophetic words.

"I was taught to run a program, not just coach a team," he told a crowd of media, fans, and players that had gathered in the Peebles Practice Facility to hear the announcement that Williams would take over as Carolina's new head basketball coach.

Entering the 2003–04 season, the Tar Heels had won a combined five NCAA Tournament games in the previous five seasons. They had missed the NCAA Tournament for two straight seasons and hadn't finished in the Associated Press top five since 1998.

And those were just the hard statistical numbers, the figures that had more to do with, as Williams put it, "coaching a team." The program-oriented facts were more painful. Summer pickup games, once the best June basketball outside of the NBA Finals, had dwindled. Players and their families spoke freely to the media about the latest perceived problems within the program. There was little organized community outreach.

The very next day, Williams began rebuilding the program's foundation, handing out Krispy Kreme doughnuts near the Old Well—one Tar Heel to another. He was the first Carolina head coach in almost 50 years to bring substantial head-coaching experience to the job, and it showed. Williams imported his entire coaching staff, a group he had hand selected. They were picked for basketball knowledge, certainly; but they were also picked for the way they formed a cohesive unit.

"We're all so different," Steve Robinson said of the staff. "You've got young, you've got old, you've got sarcasm, you've got emotional, you've got calm. We cover every aspect. At the end of the day, it's a great compliment to everybody's personality in the way all those pieces of the puzzle mesh. The guy who does the best job of meshing them is Coach Williams. He's got a little bit of all of it in him. We all bring something a little different to the table. We're

all independent thinkers. But we all care about one common thing, and that's
to try to be the best basketball program we can be at the University of North
Carolina."

In addition to a full six seasons at Carolina, every member of the staff had
had extensive previous experience with Williams. Joe Holladay joined Williams's staff at Kansas in 1993, and Robinson spent a combined eight seasons
with the Jayhawks. C.B. McGrath spent four seasons playing for Williams and
then four seasons on the staff in Lawrence. Jerod Haase played three seasons
at Kansas and also spent four seasons on the staff.

That vast experience provided the staff with a unique window into Williams's development as a head coach. He acquired a reputation as a wily veteran coach who was stuck in his ways, but in reality he had grown into a savvy
tactician who was willing to adjust to make the best use of his personnel. Call
time-outs earlier? He would do it if the situation dictated it. Play zone? Sure, if
the game circumstances required it.

Williams's adjustments weren't always in-game changes. They were sometimes more dramatic changes over the course of a season, designed to maxi-
mize a team's potential. If the head coach could change his putter after almost

three decades—he recently did, to the shock of those who know him—he could certainly change his leadership style.

"I think he's catered to the players a little more in terms of shortening practice, or maybe he's a little more accepting of injuries," McGrath said. "It's something that has happened over time. Injuries seem more common, and that may be because they work a little harder year-round than we did when I played.

"You can get the same amount done in a shorter practice as long as you are organized, and Coach is organized down to the minute. He has changed a lot that way. He is more laid back. With winning two championships, he doesn't always have to prove himself night in and night out. He's in the Hall of Fame. What else could you accomplish in a career? He's one of the most decorated coaches in a long time. I think the players feel more comfortable joking around with him. He laughs more, and that might come from age or a different staff or different players."

That's not to say that Williams is soft. Some of the players on his first Carolina team were stunned to find out that the "aw shucks, gosh darn" guy they had watched on ESPN could also be a ferocious competitor in games and practices. In his very first season, he sent Rashad McCants and Jesse Holley to the locker room before the end of a game for the egregious transgression of not taking a nonconference game seriously enough.

What players soon learned to appreciate about Williams was that their in-game mistakes never became personal. The off-court world and on-court world were two distinct areas, and he never commingled the two.

"When we're at practice, Coach doesn't talk

top: Steve Robinson going over the Duke scouting report. (Photo by Bob Leverone, *The Sporting News*)

bottom: Assistant coach Joe Holladay. (Photo by Robert Crawford)

about their academics or their social life or anything," Holladay said. "It's all business, directed toward practice and the team. Then, the minute practice is over, Coach can put that practice behind him. Before they even get to the locker room, they know Coach is just looking out for the big picture and nothing is personal. You'll never hear Coach say, 'You're stupid.' It's not a personal thing to him. It's just coaching the team and correcting a mistake. He thinks every mistake should be corrected or it becomes a permanent mistake."

That's a philosophy that sounded familiar to the legions of Carolina lettermen that had already come through the program, because it was very similar to the views of Dean Smith. Even minutes after the 2009 national title, Williams said, "The words 'Roy Williams' and 'Dean Smith' don't belong in the same sentence." But they've run the Tar Heel program in comparable ways.

Both men believe the position of head basketball coach at North Carolina comes with responsibilities beyond the hardwood. Williams has reestablished the importance of Carolina Basketball within the Chapel Hill and statewide community. The head coach and his wife, Wanda, have personally donated more than $250,000 to the Carolina Covenant, a UNC initiative that allows low-income students to attend the university debt free. The basketball program now holds an annual Special Olympics clinic, and the sale of autographed basketballs has raised over $400,000 for local charities. Williams hosts a season-opening Coaches vs. Cancer breakfast that has raised more than $500,000, and he and Wanda sponsor a sports-memorabilia auction that has raised close to $1 million to fight pediatric cancer.

top: Assistant coach C.B. McGrath. (Photo by Jim Bounds)

bottom: Joe Holladay, C.B. McGrath, and Jerod Haase have a combined 36 years on Roy Williams's staff. (Photo by Robert Crawford)

opposite: Roy Williams saluted the Tar Heel fans after winning his second NCAA title as head coach. (Photo by Streeter Lecka, Getty Images)

He's visible at dozens of Carolina athletic events every season. In December he moved a basketball practice the morning after a night game to 8:00 A.M. so he could attend the football team's bowl game. In April, on the night after winning the national title, he was there for the first pitch of a 6:00 P.M. Carolina baseball game.

The Williams and Smith worlds diverge in terms of recruiting, where Smith recruited in a four-year college basketball world and Williams often has to deal with the one-year realities. Already, two Tar Heels in the Williams era—Brandan Wright and Marvin Williams—have spent just one year in Chapel Hill before heading to the NBA, and a total of seven players in six seasons have left early for the pros.

That requires a constant replenishment of the program's talent, a situation that can create friction when a roster includes multiple All-Americas at multiple positions. So far, however, that friction has never translated to the court.

"People always wonder how Coach gets us to play so well, how he can get all these McDonald's All-Americans to play together," Ed Davis said. "But when you get here, it's so easy. Everyone is a team, and everyone pushes after that one mission. Everyone wants to win. No one was selfish, and you could never see it on someone's face in the locker room if they had a bad game or didn't get enough shots. When freshmen come in, they see how you just want to win. No one is thinking about stats. That's what Coach does. He makes it so everyone wants to win, and no one cares about who scores the most or gets the most rebounds."

The experience of testing the NBA Draft waters the previous June had exposed Danny Green, Wayne Ellington, and Ty Lawson to the world of professional basketball. But once they returned to Chapel Hill, they acknowledged it had also exposed them to the breadth and depth of the Carolina Basketball family. Before, it had been a somewhat vague idea. Now, it was specific. Now they knew that at almost every NBA interview spot, they'd been introduced as a "Carolina guy" and found that nearly every staff or administration had at least one other Carolina guy who was watching out for them.

They returned to Chapel Hill with the knowledge that Mitch Kupchak and George Karl and Donnie Walsh—individuals they previously knew only as names—were real people, real NBA decision makers who looked out for them just like a fraternity brother. It didn't mean they could coast on their Carolina credentials. But it did mean that their Carolina credentials were a legitimate entry card to the ultimate basketball destination.

NCAA CHAMPIONS

Sports Illustrated

WWW.SI.COM

Blue Crush

North Carolina Overpowers Michigan State

BY TIM LAYDEN

Tar Heels star Tyler Hansbrough manhandles Draymond Green
Photograph by John Biever

Photo by John Biever, *Sports Illustrated*

Vince Carter, Julius Peppers, Makhtar Ndiaye, and Antawn Jamison in Detroit. (Photo by Robert Crawford)

"I didn't realize how big the Carolina family was until I went through everything last summer," Green said. "It seemed like everyone I talked to was either from Carolina, graduated from Carolina, or knew somebody from Carolina. Everyone knows who you are when you're from Carolina. It let me know how deep the family goes and how widespread it is throughout the nation."

"Even if you've never met a guy, if you cross paths with someone who played at Carolina, you have a relationship," Hansbrough said. "In a way, you already know them just because you played at Carolina. That support you get from all the former players and the Carolina family is untouchable."

That's why a legion of former Tar Heels, including Vince Carter, Antawn Jamison, and even Julius Peppers, flew into Detroit for the national title game and then celebrated with the current players at the team hotel after the game. It's why Jerry Stackhouse and Michael Jordan came back for Senior Day and spent most of their time standing and clapping, cheering for the same program that had transformed them from schoolboys into basketball royalty.

Many of those players would be back in the summer of 2009, competing against the current Tar Heels in the ferocious pickup games that highlight the annual Carolina Basketball School. They'll take charges, beg for calls from the game's officials, and try to throw down nasty dunks on each other.

Because of NCAA rules, Williams can't watch those games. But word of the day's events almost always reaches him through the sweeping Carolina Basketball grapevine. He has presided over a period of unprecedented success in Chapel Hill, where dominance is expected and simple success usually not good enough. The most impressive part of his first six seasons is that he considers the wins to be only part of his job description and his stated mission—a simple declaration of where Carolina Basketball has been, where it is today, and where it's going under Williams's leadership: "Our goal here is to graduate our players," he said, "and doing it with really good kids who care about the university, who care about each other, and who have a chance to win it all."

Hoopin' with the Commander in Chief

Jack Wooten is going to need photographs, lots of them, as evidence of his remarkable two seasons as a Carolina Basketball player. A walk-on from Burlington, he parlayed two years in the junior-varsity program into an adventure that seems too good to be true. But he may need some documentation to back up his tales. They're going to be pretty good stories if anyone believes him.

Let's see: make the varsity, play in two Final Fours and win a national championship, make Phi Beta Kappa, and have not one, but two, close encounters with Barack Obama.

Yeah, right, who wouldn't believe that?

In April 2008 then-senator Obama played a pickup game for 75 minutes with the Tar Heels. Obama was in town for a rally prior to the North Carolina Democratic Primary.

The senator asked if he could play basketball with the Tar Heels, and despite a 7:00 A.M. tip time and ongoing exams, every single player on campus showed up to meet the senator.

Wooten got a call the night before while at the library studying for his final in Latin American politics. Blowing off sleep to meet the candidate was a no-brainer, and he even drew the assignment of guarding Obama during the game.

"At one point, we were discussing my exam," said Wooten. "Usually when guys are talking and the others are ready to play, someone will tell you to shut up. Funny, but this time no one said a word."

Wooten drew the ire of Roy Williams and even his teammates for defending Obama as though he were a Blue Devil. He blocked one of Obama's shots, stole the ball from him twice, and fouled him a couple of times.

"I haven't been able to get you to play defense all year and now you're stealing the ball from a guy who could audit you in a few months," cracked Williams.

The senator let Jack know how his career nearly came to an inglorious ending.

"Jack, see those guys over there [pointing to the Secret Service agents]? They were this close to taking you out." Everyone in the gym pretty much thought he was kidding.

For the Tar Heels, it was a memorable experience.

"Fifty years from now, I will still remember that day and tell people I had a chance to play basketball with a man who was the next president of the United States," said Tyler Hansbrough.

Eleven months later, Obama's and Carolina's paths crossed once again. ESPN asked the president to fill out an NCAA bracket, and he not only picked UNC to win the championship, he also threw down a challenge: "I picked you all last year—you let me down. This year, don't embarrass me in front of the nation, all right? I'm counting on you."

Nothing like some commander-in-chief-sized pressure tossed on a team that had already spent the year dealing with expectations.

"That was the cherry on top of that whole pressure situation," said Ginyard. "We all got a good laugh out of it, but we knew in our minds we were going to be 'led by our dreams and not pushed by our problems.' So it wasn't any more added pressure."

The president based his pick in part on Carolina guard Ty Lawson overcoming his well-chronicled toe injury.

"I'm going with experience, and I think Lawson is going to be healthy," the president said. "Having an experienced point guard who can control the game and make free throws at the end, that's going to be the difference."

That analysis worked out pretty well, considering Lawson made a record 25 free throws in the Final Four.

Then-senator Barack Obama played ball with the Tar Heels. (Photo by Jeffrey A. Camarati)

Jack Wooten defended Barack Obama. (Photo by Jeffrey A. Camarati)

"It was pretty cool to think this is the president, and with all he has to do to run the country, he knows a little bit about me and my game," said Lawson.

The Tar Heels received a thank-you from the nation's first fan when the team visited the White House on May 11.

"Congratulations on bringing Carolina its fifth national championship," said Obama. "And more importantly, thanks for salvaging my bracket and vindicating me before the entire nation."

The president congratulated the seniors for graduating and the team for its community service, saying that he was proud of Hansbrough for staying in school for four years and of Lawson for his outstanding play in the NCAA Tournament.

"It made me nervous to hear him say those nice things and spotlight me," said Lawson. "But it's exciting to know he appreciated the way I played in the NCAA Tournament."

Williams presented President Obama with a jersey and asked the seniors to present a signed photo of the team. The normally unflappable coach admitted to being nervous because he was unclear of the protocol.

"They tell me I am supposed to walk out with the president, but I didn't know if I was standing in the right spot or if I was supposed to say anything," said Williams. "I coached in front of 70,000-plus fans in Detroit and wasn't nervous, but my heart was racing standing there with the president."

Williams said it was the first time he's been nervous since he gave the commencement address at T. C. Roberson High School, his alma mater in Asheville, in 1992.

"As we walked into the Diplomat Room to meet the president, Marc Campbell said, 'When's the last time Coach was in a room and he was not *the* Big Shot,'" said Ginyard. "We don't get excited by much, but you could look around that room and see how excited and awestruck everyone was."

President Obama spoke highly of Williams: "What makes Coach Williams one of the great coaches isn't just his extraordinary record, but his dedication to his players. He's just as serious about making these guys into men and into leaders as he is into making them champions."

"It was very intimidating [to have] the president talk about me," said Williams. "I don't get caught up in what others say, but this is the president of the United States. It was about as nice a feeling as you can have. I could see the text he was reading from at the podium, and he did ad-lib a lot, which was nice, because that meant a speechwriter didn't say all those nice things — he did.

"President Obama is an *unintimidating*, intimidating person, which is a great quality to have. He puts you completely at ease, or at least as much as you can be when talking to the president."

The president congratulated Wooten for making Phi Beta Kappa, laughed

about his overzealous defensive effort against him in Chapel Hill, and said, "I know Jack is interested in serving our country. So Jack, any time you are ready, come on board."

"Everyone introduced themselves as he shook hands with us," Wooten said. "But when the president came to me, he said, 'Jack Wooten, the guy who blocked my shot, stole the ball, and fouled me.' Wow, what a memory."

Wooten didn't get to dress out for the Oklahoma and Michigan State games because of roster limits, but he was featured prominently in photos of both encounters with Obama.

"I was in the *New York Daily News* guarding the senator; now I am standing front and center behind the president at the White House," said Wooten. "I hated not dressing for those games, but I'd say I did okay as a Tar Heel."

And he has the photos to prove it.

Stats and Notes

2008-2009 UNC Men's Basketball Statistics

ALL 38 GAMES

Player	GP-GS	MIN	AVE	FG	FG%	3FG	3FG%	FT
Hansbrough	34–34	1029	30.3	223–434	.514	9–23	.391	249–296
Lawson	35–35	1048	29.9	182–342	.532	51–108	.472	166–208
Ellington	38–37	1155	30.4	215–445	.483	85–204	.417	87–112
Green	38–38	1040	27.4	184–391	.471	77–184	.418	52–61
Thompson	38–37	943	24.8	164–333	.492	0–0	—	73–113
Davis	38–2	716	18.8	99–191	.518	0–0	—	55–96
Graves	20–0	224	11.2	31–71	.437	10–36	.278	8–9
Zeller	15–2	117	7.8	17–36	.472	0–0	—	13–17
Frasor	38–4	662	17.4	37–111	.333	20–73	.274	6–13
Drew II	38–0	364	9.6	20–57	.351	6–26	.231	7–17
Ginyard	3–0	37	12.3	1–4	.250	0–0	—	2–4
Tanner	21–0	45	2.1	8–19	.421	5–14	.357	2–6
Moody	21–0	44	2.1	7–12	.583	0–0	—	8–13
Copeland	17–1	42	2.5	4–16	.250	0–2	.000	5–5
Watts	27–0	85	3.1	8–33	.242	0–6	.000	3–7
Wooten	19–0	37	1.9	4–11	.364	1–5	.200	1–4
Campbell	20–0	37	1.9	1–3	.333	0–1	.000	2–2
UNC	**38**	**7625**		**1205–2509**	**.480**	**264–682**	**.387**	**739–983**
Opponents	**38**	**7625**		**1013–2468**	**.410**	**274–814**	**.337**	**435–627**

NCAA TOURNAMENT GAMES

Player	GP-GS	MIN	AVE	FG	FG%	3FG	3FG%	FT
Lawson	5–5	165	33.0	28–56	.500	9–18	.500	39–51
Ellington	6–6	201	33.5	44–80	.550	17–32	.531	10–13
Hansbrough	6–6	181	30.2	32–68	.471	0–4	.000	41–53
Green	6–6	172	28.7	26–59	.441	13–30	.433	7–7
Davis	6–0	116	19.3	20–35	.571	0–0	—	9–20
Thompson	6–6	123	20.5	18–43	.419	0–0	—	6–11
Frasor	6–1	116	19.3	6–9	.667	3–4	.750	0–0
Zeller	6–0	32	5.3	5–9	.556	0–0	—	1–3
Drew II	6–0	43	7.2	3–8	.375	1–4	.250	0–3
Copeland	5–0	12	2.4	2–9	.222	0–0	—	1–1
Watts	5–0	18	3.6	1–3	.333	0–0	—	0–0
Campbell	3–0	4	1.3	0–1	.000	0–0	—	0–0
Tanner	4–0	9	2.3	0–3	.000	0–2	.000	0–0
Moody	3–0	4	1.3	0–1	.000	0–0	—	0–0
Wooten	2–0	4	2.0	0–1	.000	0–0	—	0–0
UNC	**6**	**1200**		**185–385**	**.481**	**43–94**	**.457**	**114–162**
Opponents	**6**	**1200**		**150–390**	**.385**	**35–131**	**.267**	**71–104**

FT%	OFF	DEF	REB	AVE	PF	A	TO	BL	ST	PTS	AVE
.841	103	173	276	8.1	77	34	63	12	42	704	20.7
.798	23	81	104	3.0	59	230	66	5	75	581	16.6
.777	57	129	186	4.9	57	101	62	6	36	602	15.8
.852	70	108	178	4.7	84	104	63	51	67	497	13.1
.646	70	146	216	5.7	85	26	48	40	35	401	10.6
.573	83	167	250	6.6	74	22	40	65	14	253	6.7
.889	22	29	51	2.6	32	15	23	2	7	80	4.0
.765	11	19	30	2.0	20	3	8	3	3	47	3.1
.462	23	52	75	2.0	52	54	26	5	22	100	2.6
.412	5	36	41	1.1	36	74	45	1	15	53	1.4
.500	6	2	8	2.7	5	4	3	0	2	4	1.3
.333	2	5	7	0.3	4	1	1	0	1	23	1.1
.615	4	11	15	0.7	7	0	3	3	2	22	1.0
1.000	4	9	13	0.8	8	1	2	0	0	13	0.8
.429	7	13	20	0.7	6	5	9	3	2	19	0.7
.250	0	5	5	0.3	1	2	2	0	0	10	0.5
1.000	1	4	5	0.3	2	9	7	0	2	4	0.2
.752	**556**	**1041**	**1597**	**42.0**	**609**	**685**	**472**	**196**	**325**	**3413**	**89.9**
.694	**494**	**863**	**1357**	**35.7**	**785**	**518**	**605**	**167**	**266**	**2735**	**72.0**

FT%	OFF	DEF	REB	AVE	PF	A	TO	BL	ST	PTS	AVE
.765	2	19	21	4.2	8	34	7	1	16	104	20.8
.769	8	26	34	5.7	5	16	13	2	2	115	19.2
.774	13	34	47	7.8	15	8	14	0	14	105	17.5
1.000	12	16	28	4.7	16	16	6	8	11	72	12.0
.450	10	23	33	5.5	14	1	2	8	3	49	8.2
.545	5	15	20	3.3	17	4	7	4	3	42	7.0
—	7	11	18	3.0	12	6	4	1	5	15	2.5
.333	4	10	14	2.3	6	1	2	1	0	11	1.8
.000	1	3	4	0.7	5	6	1	0	0	7	1.2
1.000	2	2	4	0.8	1	0	0	0	0	5	1.0
—	1	3	4	0.8	0	2	3	0	0	2	0.4
—	0	1	1	0.3	0	0	1	0	0	0	0.0
—	0	0	0	0.0	1	1	0	0	0	0	0.0
—	1	2	3	1.0	0	0	1	0	0	0	0.0
—	0	1	1	0.5	0	0	1	0	0	0	0.0
.704	**73**	**170**	**243**	**40.5**	**100**	**95**	**62**	**25**	**54**	**527**	**87.8**
.683	**87**	**151**	**238**	**39.7**	**126**	**61**	**94**	**23**	**34**	**406**	**67.7**

2008–2009 Game-by-Game Results

Overall record—34–4; **ACC**—13–3
Home—14–1; **Away**—8–2; **Neutral Sites**—12–1
Maui Invitational—3–0; **ACC Tournament**—1–1; **NCAA Tournament**—6–0

NOVEMBER

Day	Opponent	Site	W/L	Score	Leading Scorer	Leading Rebounder	Leading Assists
15	Penn	Home	W	86–71	Zeller 18	Davis 14	Ellington, Lawson 5
18	Kentucky	Home	W	77–58	Thompson 20	Davis 10	Lawson 9
21	UC Santa Barbara	Away	W	84–67	Lawson 19	Thompson 10	Frasor 3
24	Chaminade	Maui-1	W	115–70	Green 26	Davis 8	Drew II 7
25	Oregon	Maui-1	W	98–69	Green 21	Davis 13	Drew II, Lawson 5
26	Notre Dame	Maui-1	W	102–87	Hansbrough 34	Thompson 13	Lawson 11
30	UNC Asheville	Home	W	116–48	Lawson 22	Davis 10	Lawson 8

DECEMBER

Day	Opponent	Site	W/L	Score	Leading Scorer	Leading Rebounder	Leading Assists
3	Michigan State	Detroit-2	W	98–63	Hansbrough 25	Hansbrough 11	Lawson 8
13	Oral Roberts	Home	W	100–84	Hansbrough 26	Hansbrough 9	Lawson 7
18	Evansville	Home	W	91–73	Hansbrough 20	Davis 10	Lawson 6
21	Valparaiso	Chicago	W	85–63	Hansbrough 25	Thompson 6	Ellington, Lawson 5
28	Rutgers	Home	W	97–75	Hansbrough 26	Hansbrough 10	Lawson 6
31	Nevada	Away	W	84–61	Hansbrough 22	Davis 8	Lawson 7

JANUARY

Day	Opponent	Site	W/L	Score	Leading Scorer	Leading Rebounder	Leading Assists
4	Boston College	Home	L	78–85	Hansbrough 21	Hansbrough 9	Lawson 4
7	C of Charleston	Home	W	108–70	Hansbrough 24	Davis, Hansbrough 7	Lawson 8
11	Wake Forest	Away	L	89–92	Green 22	Hansbrough 11	Lawson 5
15	Virginia	Away	W	83–61	Hansbrough 28	Hansbrough 12	Lawson 9
17	Miami	Home	W	82–65	Hansbrough 24	Davis, Thompson 8	Lawson 8
21	Clemson	Home	W	94–70	Ellington 25	Hansbrough 10	Ellington, Lawson 7
28	Florida State	Away	W	80–77	Lawson 21	Lawson 9	Lawson 4
31	NC State	Away	W	93–76	Hansbrough 31	Davis, Thompson 7	Lawson 5

FEBRUARY

Day	Opponent	Site	W/L	Score	Leading Scorer	Leading Rebounder	Leading Assists
3	Maryland	Home	W	108-91	Ellington 34	Ellington 9	Lawson 6
7	Virginia	Home	W	76–61	Ellington 20	Hansbrough 13	Lawson 9
11	Duke	Away	W	101–87	Lawson 25	Ellington 7	Lawson 5
15	Miami	Away	W	69–65	Lawson 21	Davis 11	Ellington 5
18	NC State	Home	W	89–80	Hansbrough 27	Hansbrough 7	Lawson 9
21	Maryland	Away	L (ot)	85–88	Lawson 24	Hansbrough 11	Lawson 2
28	Georgia Tech	Home	W	104–74	Hansbrough 28	Hansbrough 10	Lawson 11

MARCH

Day	Opponent	Site	W/L	Score	Leading Scorer	Leading Rebounder	Leading Assists
4	Virginia Tech	Away	W	86–78	Hansbrough, Lawson 22	Hansbrough 15	Lawson 5
8	Duke	Home	W	79–71	Hansbrough 17	Hansbrough, Lawson 8	Lawson 9
13	Virginia Tech	Atlanta-3	W	79–76	Hansbrough 28	Hansbrough 8	Drew II, Ellington 4
14	Florida State	Atlanta-3	L	70–73	Ellington 24	Hansbrough 11	Drew II, Ellington 3
19	Radford	Greensboro-4	W	101–58	Ellington 25	Green 10	Drew II 5
21	LSU	Greensboro-4	W	84–70	Ellington, Lawson 23	Hansbrough 8	Lawson 6
27	Gonzaga	Memphis-5	W	98–77	Hansbrough 24	Hansbrough 10	Lawson 9
29	Oklahoma	Memphis-5	W	72–60	Lawson 19	Hansbrough 6	Lawson 5

APRIL

Day	Opponent	Site	W/L	Score	Leading Scorer	Leading Rebounder	Leading Assists
4	Villanova	Detroit-6	W	83–69	Lawson 22	Hansbrough 11	Lawson 8
6	Michigan State	Detroit-6	W	89–72	Lawson 21	Davis 8	Lawson 6

NEUTRAL-SITE KEY

1 — EA Sports Maui Invitational, Lahaina, Maui
2 — ACC/Big Ten Challenge, Detroit, Mich.
3 — ACC Tournament, Atlanta, Ga.
4 — NCAA Tournament, Greensboro, N.C.
5 — NCAA South Regional, Memphis, Tenn.
6 — NCAA Final Four, Detroit, Mich.

2008–2009 Postseason Notes

The Tar Heels won a school-best 70 games over the last two seasons. (Photo by Jeffrey A. Camarati)

Carolina has won NCAA Tournament titles in 1957, 1982, 1993, 2005, and 2009. The 17-point margin of victory over Michigan State was greater than the combined margins in the Tar Heels' first four NCAA titles (13 total points—one in 1957, one in 1982, six in 1993, and five in 2005).

Roy Williams became the fourth active coach and 13th all time to win two or more NCAA championships, leading UNC to the title in 2005 and 2009. Williams was an assistant under Dean Smith when the Tar Heels won the title in 1982. Smith won a second title in 1993.

Carolina's five NCAA titles ties them with Indiana for third place. UCLA (11) and Kentucky (7) are the only schools with more.

Carolina played in the Final Four for an NCAA-record 18th time and ninth time in the last 19 years.

Roy Williams has led teams at North Carolina and Kansas to seven Final Fours. He is fourth in NCAA history behind John Wooden, Dean Smith, and Mike Krzyzewski.

The Tar Heels have played in the Final Four three times in the last five years. No other ACC school has reached a regional final in those five years. Carolina is 20–3 in the NCAA Tournament in the last five years. The rest of the ACC is 20–22 in the NCAA Tournament during that span.

Carolina was seeded number one in the South Regional, the 13th time the Tar Heels have earned a top seed in the NCAA Tournament. No other school has been a No. 1 seed more than 10 times.

The national championship game was Carolina's 102nd victory in 141 NCAA Tournament games. The 102 wins are more than any other school in the country. Kentucky is second with 98.

Roy Williams is 55–18 in NCAA Tournament games. He is third in NCAA Tournament victories, second among active coaches.

The Tar Heels led Michigan State 55–34 at halftime. The 55 points were the most scored in the first half in championship-game history, and the 21-point lead was the largest halftime advantage ever in the finals.

Carolina became the first team to win six games by at least 12 points in the same NCAA Tournament. The closest margin was a 72–60 win over Oklahoma in the regional final.

UNC trailed for a combined 9:50 in the six NCAA games, including 7:15 in the second round against LSU. The Tigers led nine times—three times in the second half, including one stretch of 4:03 in which they built a 54–49 lead with just over 12 minutes to play. Gonzaga led twice in the first two minutes for 46 seconds; Villanova led three times for 1:30, but the Wildcats did not lead after the 16:57 mark of the first half; and Michigan State led one time for 19 seconds before the Tar Heels took the lead for good on a Danny Green three-pointer 1:08 into the game.

Danny Green finished his career among UNC leaders in blocks, three-pointers, and free-throw percentage. (Photo by Jack Morton)

Carolina went 34–4 overall, tying the second-most wins in a season in school history. The 2006–07, 2007–08, and 2008–09 teams mark the first time the Tar Heels have won 30 or more games in three consecutive seasons.

This was the 10th 30-win season in UNC history. Duke also has 10 30-win seasons. The rest of the ACC has a combined three (one each by Maryland, NC State, and Virginia). Roy Williams has led the Tar Heels to four 30-wins seasons and has nine overall (the second most in NCAA history).

Carolina has finished in the top 10 in the Associated Press poll in each of the last five years. That is the first time UNC has accomplished that since Dean Smith's teams did it nine straight years from 1981 to 1989.

The Tar Heels went 13–3 in ACC play, winning the regular-season title for an unprecedented 27th time. No other school has more than 18. Roy Williams has led the Tar Heels to four ACC regular-season crowns in his six seasons as head coach.

The Tar Heels are 81–28 against ACC opponents in the last six seasons, including a 33–15 record in ACC road games. Duke is second in road wins in that time with 31. No other ACC school has won more than 17 on the road in the last six years.

Danny Green set Carolina career records for most games played (145) and most wins (123). He is tied for second in ACC history in wins. Green is the only player in ACC history with 1,000 points, 500 rebounds, 250 assists, 150 three-pointers, 150 blocks, and 150 steals. The North Babylon, New York, native is third in Carolina history in free-throw percentage (.845) and eighth in both blocked shots (155) and three-pointers (184).

The 2009 senior class (Mike Copeland, Bobby Frasor, Marcus Ginyard, Danny Green, and Tyler Hansbrough) set a four-year UNC record by winning 124 games. Green and Hansbrough set the UNC record by playing in 58 ACC wins (regular season and tournament).

- Most Outstanding Player of the 2009 Final Four, scoring 39 points (19.5 per game) and grabbing 13 rebounds (6.5 per game) in the wins over Villanova and Michigan State
- Scored 17 first-half points in national championship game win over Michigan State, helping the Tar Heels sprint to a 55–34 halftime lead (the most points ever in the first half by a team in the national championship game)
- Was 7 for 9 from the floor and 3 for 3 from behind the arc in the opening half
- Made five three-pointers, scored 20 points, and grabbed nine rebounds against Villanova in the national semifinals
- Joins a list of Tar Heel Final Four MVPs that includes James Worthy (1982), Donald Williams (1993), and Sean May (2005)
- Set Final Four record for highest three-point percentage as he made 8 of 10 threes (80%), breaking the previous Final Four mark of 71.4 set by UNC's Donald Williams in 1993 (Williams made 10 of 14)
- Finished his career 18th in UNC scoring with 1,694 points, an average of 14.7 per game
- Scored 20 or more points in four of his last seven games, including three consecutive postseason games (Florida State, Radford, and LSU), the first time he accomplished that
- Made 229 three-pointers, the second most in UNC history
- Earned All-ACC Tournament honors in three seasons (first team in 2007 and 2008, second team in 2009)
- Carolina was 52–0 in his career when he shot 50% or better from the floor
- Averaged 19.2 points and 5.7 rebounds in the 2009 NCAA Tournament, shooting 55.0% from the floor (44 of 80) and 17 of 32 from three-point range (.531)

top: Wayne Ellington is second all time at Carolina with 229 three-point baskets. (Photo by Brian Fleming)

bottom: Ellington was a first-round draft pick of the Minnesota Timberwolves. (Photo by Jack Morton)

TY LAWSON

- Won the 2009 Bob Cousy Award presented by the Basketball Hall of Fame as the best point guard in the country
- Was the ACC Player of the Year, the NCAA South Regional Most Outstanding Player, and a member of the 2009 Final Four All-Tournament Team
- The 18th Tar Heel, and the first UNC point guard, to win NCAA regional MVP honors
- First point guard to win ACC Player of the Year honors since Carolina's Phil Ford in 1978
- First-team All-America by the NABC, the Los Angeles Athletic Club (Wooden), *Sports Illustrated*, CBS Sportsline.com, and *Basketball Times*; second-team by the Associated Press, *Sporting News*, and Rupp; third-team by Fox
- USBWA District 3 Player of the Year
- Career assist-error ratio of 2.78, second in ACC history
- In five games in the 2009 NCAA Tournament, averaged a team-high 20.8 points; shot 50% from the floor (28 for 56), 50% from three-point range (9 for 18), and 76.5% from the free-throw line (39 for 51); and had 34 assists, 7 turnovers, and 16 steals
- Had 43 points (21.5 average), 14 assists (7.0), 5 turnovers (2.5), and 10 steals (5.0) in the Final Four
- Set Final Four records for most free throws attempted (35) and made (25)
- Led all players on both teams with 21 points and eight steals (set championship game record) and added six assists and one turnover in the NCAA championship game win over Michigan State
- Had seven steals in the first half as UNC shot 52.9% from the floor and built a 55–34 lead
- Led the ACC in 2009 in assists (230, 6.6 per game), assist-error (3.49), and steals (75, 2.14 per game)
- First point guard ever to lead UNC in field-goal percentage
- Had 230 assists and only 66 turnovers in 2009, an assist-error ratio of 3.49 that is the best in ACC history
- MVP at the 2008 Maui Invitational

top: Ty Lawson was sensational in NCAA play, including the championship game versus Michigan State. (Photo by Jeffrey A. Camarati)

left: Lawson was the 18th player selected in the first round of the 2009 NBA Draft. (Photo by Jeffrey A. Camarati)

right: Michael Jordan and Lawson — two Tar Heels with NCAA championships. (Photo by Jeffrey A. Camarati)

TYLER HANSBROUGH

- Four-time first-team All-America, the only player in ACC history to accomplish that
- Four-time first-team All-ACC selection, the only player in ACC history to accomplish that
- First in ACC and 12th in NCAA history with 2,872 points
- Set the ACC career scoring record with 22 points against Radford in the first round of the 2009 NCAA Tournament
- Carolina's all-time leading scorer in NCAA Tournament play with 325 points—fourth most in NCAA history behind only Christian Laettner, Elvin Hayes, and Danny Manning
- Holds NCAA career record for made free throws (982) and is second all time in free-throw attempts (1,241)
- The 2008 National Player of the Year, ACC Player of the Year, ACC Male Athlete of the Year, ACC Tournament MVP, NCAA East Regional Player of the Year
- Consensus first-team All-America in 2007, 2008, and 2009—the 14th three-time consensus All-America since World War II and the first since Oklahoma's Wayman Tisdale and Georgetown's Patrick Ewing in 1985
- Associated Press (second time), USBWA (third time), and *The Sporting News* (fourth time) first-team All-America in 2009
- Only player in ACC history to lead his school in scoring and rebounding for four seasons
- Became the 13th player in ACC history and the first Tar Heel to earn first-team All-ACC Tournament honors three times
- Third Tar Heel (with J.R. Reid, 1987–89; and Ed Cota, 1997, 1998, and 2000) to earn a spot on All-NCAA Regional Team in three seasons
- Set the ACC record for career 20-point games (78, breaking Duke's J.J. Redick's mark of 70)
- Set the ACC record for career double-figure games with 133 (previous mark of 129 held by Duke's Johnny Dawkins)
- Broke Sam Perkins's UNC rebounding record (finished with 1,219)
- Will be the eighth Tar Heel to have his jersey (#50) retired and the first since Antawn Jamison, who played his final season in 1997–98 (Jack Cobb, #10 Lennie Rosenbluth, #12 Phil Ford, #20 George Glamack, #23 Michael Jordan, #33 Jamison, and #52 James Worthy)

No other Tar Heel will again wear the number 50 made famous by Hansbrough. (Photo by Robert Crawford)

- Averaged 20.2 points, the sixth-highest average in UNC history
- One of four finalists for the 2008 James E. Sullivan Award as the top amateur athlete in the country

Hansbrough helped Carolina achieve:

- A 120–22 record overall—50–14 in ACC regular-season play, 8–2 in ACC Tournament action, and 14–3 in the NCAA Tournament
- Three consecutive number-one seeds in the NCAA Tournament (and a number three in 2006), two Final Fours (2008 and 2009), and the 2009 NCAA title
- Three consecutive ACC regular-season championships
- Final Associated Press rankings of number 10 in 2006, number four in 2007, number one in 2008, and number two in 2009
- 57–8 record at the Smith Center
- A 25–7 ACC road record, including 14–2 in the last two years and a 4–0 record at Duke

Acknowledgments

Four years ago, Adam Lucas, Matt Bowers, and I wrote a book about the 2005 national championship. Adam is a gifted storyteller who publishes *Tar Heel Monthly*, and Matt has teamed with me at UNC athletic communications covering basketball for the past 10 years. It took us almost a month to come up with the title, *Led by Their Dreams*. Adam hit upon it after a marathon interview session with Roy Williams. As we walked to our cars, he mentioned the phrase, which Coach Williams likes to use when talking to his players in pressure-filled situations. We went with it.

Fast forward to Ford Field, April 6, 2009. Actually, April 7, because this time it took us only until Williams's press conference, held just after midnight, to come up with the title for this year's book.

One Fantastic Ride—it's a phrase I first heard Anson Dorrance use as he walked off the field after one of the many national championships won by his Carolina women's soccer team. Dorrance and Williams are a lot alike. Both are Carolina graduates and known for their competitive nature, recruiting acumen, and ability to relate to young people. They also have reached remarkable levels of success and stand at the top of their professions.

Williams and Dorrance are emphatic about their players "enjoying the journey" during their college careers and hope that they will look back fondly and say what a blast they had along the way.

Well, we've been fortunate to work with Carolina Basketball for a number of years and can say unequivocally that the 2008–09 Tar Heels were a blast to be around and watch as they reached their championship dreams.

We witnessed things that most of Carolina Nation couldn't, such as the stoic maturity of freshman Tyler Zeller as he sat in the training room realizing that his season might have ended after just two games because of a broken wrist; the players acting like any other college kids jumping off the Maui cliffs into the Pacific Ocean; the pride in the locker room after the senior class had completed its 4–0 sweep at Duke; the anger and frustration of the players after losing at Maryland; and the deep happiness and sense of accomplishment after winning it all in Detroit. We hope our unique access allows you to enjoy the season more thoroughly.

We thank the players, coaches, and staff for granting us almost 25 hours of interviews. Getting an opportunity to see Wayne Ellington's smile grow wider and wider as he talked about the NCAA Tournament, watch Tyler Hansbrough get fired up talking about the Duke and NC State rivalries, and hear Deon Thompson share his feelings about Coach Williams were moments we will never forget.

left: An unforgettable
senior class: Mike
Copeland, Marcus
Ginyard, Tyler
Hansbrough, Danny
Green, and Bobby
Frasor. (Photo by
Jeffrey A. Camarati)

right: Tyler Hansbrough
(left) and Wayne
Ellington were all
smiles after beating
Michigan State. (Photo
by Jeffrey A. Camarati)

Thanks to Ken Cleary, Jason Andrews, and the staff at UNC New Media for manning the camera and David Culp, Lauren Brownlow, and the students in athletic communications for transcribing the interviews.

A special thanks to director of athletic photography Jeffrey Camarati for his wonderful work, including his preparation of the more than 200 photos included in this keepsake. Thanks also to photographers J. D. Lyon Jr., Jim Hawkins, Robert Crawford, Bob Donnan, Peyton Williams, Jack Morton, Jim Bounds, Brian Fleming, Bob Leverone at *The Sporting News*, Getty Images, and others for allowing us to share their artistry with you.

Thanks to Tobacco Road Media; UNC Press, Mark Simpson-Vos, and Jay Mazzocchi; and Carolina's director of athletics, Dick Baddour, and marketing director, Rick Steinbacher, for putting this project together.

And finally, thanks to our families for allowing us to spend so much time on this fantastic ride: Crystal, Sam, and Chloe Bowers; Stephanie, McKay, and Asher Lucas; and Jeanne, Ryan, and Emilie Kirschner.

Hopefully, we can do this again. It really is a blast.

—STEVE KIRSCHNER